BELIEVE ME, I WAS THERE

Behind the scenes as an Arab TV Reporter

Hacene Zitouni

authorHOUSE®

AuthorHouse™ UK Ltd.
1663 Liberty Drive
Bloomington, IN 47403 USA
www.authorhouse.co.uk
Phone: 0800.197.4150

Published by AuthorHouse 08/28/2014

ISBN: 978-1-4969-8672-6 (sc)
ISBN: 978-1-4969-8671-9 (hc)
ISBN: 978-1-4969-8676-4 (e)

Contents

This book is dedicated, with deep gratitude, to all the valued colleagues and mentors who are mentioned in these pages; and to my son Atlas, who makes me very proud.

If life is a journey, then travel it well...

Foreword

I'm a foreign correspondent on TV. My job requires skill, and it can change lives.

When you've seen a TV reporter interviewing stars at the Oscars, maybe even when you've seen one talking from a rooftop while shells explode in the city below, you may have thought 'that looks easy.' They just dream up a couple of questions or some sentences of news - it's no more skilled than making a selfie with a video camera. And TV is sometimes done just like a selfie, with a 'video journalist' expected to do the cameraman's job as well. It's cheap for the TV station. But it's moribund. It's a bit like taking still pictures with a point-and-shoot camera. They're technically adequate and often good, but you hoped the result would express a lot more than it does.

Can foreign correspondents make a difference? Of course. People like me can expose injustice. On countless occasions, reports from war or famine or disaster zones have been the starting-point of humanitarian efforts that have changed lives.

Good television means collaborating. You rely on teamwork in the production team, and on a wider scale, teamwork at the TV station itself. The engineers would have no programmes to produce if it wasn't for the producers, and the producers would look pretty silly if they made a film they couldn't transmit. The journalist on the screen is just a tiny part of it.

I'm writing about the lessons I've learned, for people who want to play that tiny part: to do journalism on TV, especially Arab TV, in which I have over twenty years' experience. In Arab TV women, and less often men, are getting on-camera jobs because they look good, not because they're competent. That's insulting to women in general, and it makes those individuals vulnerable. You don't have to be good-looking to be a TV reporter, but you do need to be sensitive and quick to learn. You need to be curious about all kinds of people and places. You should be interested in politics, economics and world affairs, and to have a personal hinterland - a deeper understanding of music, or sport, or architecture for instance. You'll need self-confidence and skill in debate; whatever happens, you mustn't lose your temper. You have to be able to write economically and fast.

Be objective. You will encounter events and people who conflict with your pre-conceived opinions, and it's your job to report on them however foolish or nasty they may seem.

For your own sake, start with a career plan and be flexible enough to change it in response to opportunity. Make yourself fluent in at least one foreign language.

Finally, have courage, patience and above all – integrity: a combination of honesty, sincerity and willingness to match words with action. Integrity is the quality that will serve you best, and you'll find it's often tested.

Hacene Zitouni

London, 2014

Chapter 1

Syria, 2013

'What's my *story*? You want to know what my story is, my friend?'

I nodded, and held the microphone a bit closer to the young man to cut the hubbub outside. Nasir at my side was filming him, head and shoulders; we were all standing up. There was about six inches of headroom, and cold sunshine filtered by tent-cloth. Cloth-wrapped bundles of clothes and cooking pots were stacked against the canvas walls.

'My story is short. You come with this camera, you spend five minutes here, you're gone. On your way out you will see my house - a hundred yards from here through the olive grove. My house is empty. My land is a desert. My life is destroyed. Take your time. Have a look, this is how we live. Think what it means to be cheated.'

'Cheated?'

'Of course cheated!' His voice rose. 'They said we'd be free, like in Tunisia - no more Ben Ali. In Egypt they're free, no more Mubarak! So we've got to avenge the honour of Syria. No more Bashar al Assad, they said. Two weeks of fighting and then we can all go home. So we come over here to wait. They talked about freedom and we lapped it up, like babies –'

'Who talked about it?'

He was becoming increasingly agitated, waving his arms, talking faster; I kept the mic close. 'You know! These jerks from Idleb. City people, students, fighters, big brave nobodies - I tell you by the blood of the Prophet that these people know *nothing*. Bashar's not like Ben Ali, he's not Mubarak. He's got a vicious army and vicious police right behind him. Women and children are getting killed - bombs, and guns, we had the power cut off - and there was no water so we had to leave. We have to eat. We were at home, we had a beautiful life, my children in school –' Suddenly catching sight of a child's book, he flung it across the room. 'I'll tell you why we're here. For their convenience. So that *the brave fighters* don't have to worry about us. UNHCR and Islamic Relief have to feed us and we won't get in the line of fire.'

'You can't go home?'

I flinched at the look he gave me. Beside me I could sense Nasir rapidly pulling out from the head-and-shoulders. Still talking, the man seized a radio and hurled it across the tent. 'If we go home my children starve to death. The water's off and what are we going to eat? We stay in this slum to get this' - he picked up a bag of rice in both hands and hurled it to the ground. 'My animals are dying. My goats are eaten by gangsters. The sheep are gone - If I farm my land they say I support the Allawites. If I live in my farm' he picked up a clock – 'they smash it - like this! Now we have no money. No school. No life. They have done this to my CHILDREN!' he shouted.

He turned and seized a camping-gaz canister.

'Thank you,' I said, backing towards the entrance. 'Thank you,' muttered Nasir, and shut down.

The man was right. We come, we show what we see, we leave. Reporters can prise grief from strangers, display it to the world and go home to a comfy bed. We live with internal conflict - 'This is awful!' on one side and

'What a great image!' on the other. Like surgeons, we have to control our emotions, to be dispassionate so that we can do a job efficiently. Maybe even increase the sum of human knowledge.

And we're fast. We were at that refugee camp for just two hours before we left, safe and free, in a convoy of Islamic relief trucks that rocked out through cold chalky puddles under a deep blue sky.

Emotion, especially sickening, distressing emotion with an edge of fury physically expressed, makes excellent television. It makes you watch, goggle eyed. It makes you think, *Glad that's not me*, and *Poor fellow*. With a prompt, it makes you think *What can I do to help?*

Watching the footage of the man who went berserk in his tent, I began to edit it on my laptop, speeding along in the back of a people-carrier. There were nine people from MBC - small crews from Dubai, Ankara, Washington, and Nasir and me from London. I built my story around the whole generation of children who were out of school.

We skirted the city of Idleb, which is near to the Turkish border and not far from Aleppo, and crossed blue-green hills to the next camp. There were several within the city's radius; all much the same, long lines of greyish tents sheltering tens of thousands of IDPs - internally displaced persons; men without work, driven to the limits of mental endurance like our interviewee; toddlers playing in the dust; and women - women everywhere with faces covered, cooking on smokey camping stoves, or stepping between the puddles with plastic water carriers on their shoulders, or pegging wet laundry on ropes between the tents. Women had a domestic structure to their days. The men and children had none, so the men became embittered, while the women were simply miserable. Wherever we stopped, crowds of skinny children appeared from nowhere. Who knew what would become of them?

That spring, in the third year of conflict between the Assad regime and the Free Syrian Army, Syria still seemed relatively uncomplicated to most western media. CNN, the BBC and the rest were rooting for the rebels, who seemed just like them. (It took a while to recognise that this was an illusion.) The regime's side wasn't much reported but always implicitly condemned. The geopolitical reasons why American and European media were one-sided, and Russian media other-sided, were rarely made clear. TV is good at emotion but not always brilliant at conveying a complex political hinterland.

At the time, I wasn't thinking about this. I was telling a human-interest story: letting MBC viewers know what happened to their huge donations to Islamic Relief. Nasir and I had filmed blankets, medical supplies and boxes of food being loaded into trucks in Birmingham and we'd interviewed the helpers involved. We'd followed those trucks to Turkey, where Turks took over as drivers and led us into Syria itself.

It was early afternoon when our convoy drove into Idleb, an ancient hilltop city, rebel-held and therefore bearing signs of air attack and blast damage. We stopped at every checkpoint to have our accreditation read by scruffy fighters with sub-machine guns. The official hospitals were closed because wounded rebels would be sitting targets for air attack. Instead Islamic Relief had to deliver medical supplies to makeshift medical stations in unlikely places. The one that sticks in my mind was down an alleyway. It must have been a lovely place once; not very big, but as in any old town house, you passed through a gate in a wall into a courtyard with rooms leading off it. The street outside was full of people - nearly all men, shouting, some waving pistols, around a battered car that had arrived just before us. The crowd let us through with a tripod and the camera. Three men were dragging a heavy man with a bloody shirt out of the back seat. 'He's dead -' somebody muttered. I heard a woman say 'They caught him at the phone shop'.

Nasir had had the camera running when he stepped out of the Toyota, and filmed the slumped body being hauled through the gate, across the yard and the house. We followed. They dumped it on the floor of an empty room which was immediately flooded by spectators. A doctor with a stethoscope knelt over the man's blood-soaked chest, trying to get people to shut up so that he could listen. We sidled respectfully out. It was our job to find someone who was alive and could talk to us. Everywhere was chaos; in some of the rooms there were doctors talking German, American volunteers asking for antiseptic, the victim's old mother wailing in a corner.

A local surgeon looked as if he hadn't slept for a month. I shoved the microphone in front of him. 'We ran out of antiseptic weeks ago. We're desperate for surgical gloves and soap. We have no antibiotics. Infection is a huge problem for us. And we need an anaesthetist –'

'How many surgeons do you have here?'

'Me when I can get here, two doctors today but usually only one, one nurse and volunteers. Sometimes with unrealistic expectations.'

'But you fix people up?'

'Somehow,' he sighed 'but they come back. All they ever want to do is get back into the fight.'

There were chaotic scenes upstairs; surgical instruments had just arrived. The sterile packs were inside Islamic Relief boxes with their symbol of the dome and two minarets surmounting the globe. The moment a box reached a doctor it'd be torn open and the scalpels or tweezers, needles or speculae, put to use. On the way out we passed the door of the room where the corpse had been taken. The rabble of hangers-on had vanished but the doctor was still there, and inserting a tube into the 'corpse' whose eyes were flickering open.

We went in for a closer look. 'I was sure he was a goner,' I murmured, as the doctor tore sterile wipes from a fresh box to clean his hands.

'No,' he said. 'That's just the way things are here. Drama, always drama. He is the luckiest man in Syria - it's a flesh wound in the neck and a bullet in the shoulder. The shock knocked him out.....So when's Obama coming to help us, then?'

It's complicated.

5

Surely, nothing can be more important than a man and his wife and children being forced to live in a refugee camp when they could get by, with help, in their old home?

Perhaps only orphaned children, grieving adults, ancient mosques smashed, ruined streets, amputees, starvation, disease and poisoning – that might be more important. But these are the usual side-effects of a quarrel between Obama, Putin, King Abdullah, Netanyahu, Rafsanjani and Nasrallah. A quarrel that will be argued out, sometimes by proxy, in Geneva, New York, Jerusalem, Riyadh, Beirut, Moscow, Washington...

The Heads of State and their flunkeys won't come to Idleb, but they won't be missed. People in the camps don't think very often about them, either.

Because the Arab Spring has turned into the Arab Hell; and it's a hall of mirrors.

The Arab Spring that began early in 2011 was supposed to mean new hope, free speech, democracy, real change and no more dictatorship. In Tunisia, angry liberals were hijacked by an Islamic opposition party that had been around for years. In Cairo the Facebook generation demanded democracy, freedom of expression and liberty for women, and were so busy tweeting the latest from Tahrir Square that they didn't notice they were leaderless. The next thing they knew, the Muslim Brotherhood had taken over; they didn't last long because people were impatient for change, and now the army are back and nastier than ever.

In Syria, ordinary people bought the same old story. 'Get out of our way, and we'll get rid of the Allawite dictator. Then everybody, Sunni, Shi'a, Armenian Christians and ordinary Allawites will have a voice; everyone will get a fair share of everything, in the best of all possible worlds.' When the Syrian dictator reacted with bombs and poison gas, extreme repression was answered by extreme terrorism. Al Nusra, which claims association with Al Qaeda, and Iranian suicide bombers rode in on the side of the

Free Syrian Army. Since these extremists demand Shari'a law this didn't suit everyone, and the opposition were soon fighting like rats in a sack.

Many countries, for various reasons, had supplied the Free Syrian Army, but once the opposition got infiltrated by Iran and Hezbollah they faltered, suspecting that they'd fallen into a trap. It seemed that these newcomers, these terrorists, were ultimately on the side of Assad.

Did they *know*? The guys on the ground, the ones who were yelling *God is Great*! before blowing themselves up along with hundreds of innocent bystanders? I very much doubt it. I saw some boys from Al Nusra, which demands total war against the US and Israel, hanging out with rebel forces. A British Asian one, slung about with AK-47 and bandolier, told me in broad Yorkshire 'I won't be interviewed on camera but I'm with the rebels and what I want is the end of every dictatorship in the Muslim world.' When Bashar blamed 'foreign terrorists' he was visibly right; you could see foreigners everywhere, fighting or in support. I thought they were being conned, and simply thought they were saving Syrians from a bullying, godless régime.

As to the people in the camps, all they knew was that that the West supported the opposition and without Russian help Bashar Al Assad would be done for. That was true enough. The Syrians host an important Russian naval base and are deeply indebted to them for enormous arms sales. Putin was still smarting over money Russia had to write off when Saddam fell, not to mention a fortune in debt when Gaddafi was ousted; but the Russians had not used their veto at the UN to prevent Western intervention in Iraq or Libya. Syria was the place where Putin finally drew a line.

But Syria also has strong links with Iran, and if the West ever succeeds in breaking the link between Damascus and Teheran then Hezbollah, based in Beirut, will be significantly weakened. Iran is Hezbollah's strongest ally in maintaining its presence in Lebanon.

The geopolitics, then, is all about protecting, or alternatively breaking, a strategic link: isolating Iran from Hezbollah. The break is vital for, among others, the United States, the United Kingdom, France, Israel and Saudi Arabia.

But the Russians and Chinese, in their own economic interest, protect the link by continuing to support Iran and Syria.

As I write, a year after that visit to Idleb, it is clear to everyone that Syrian civil war is far bigger than any mere internal conflict. Russia and America remain head-to-head on this, and their battleground happens to be a once beautiful, fertile, ancient land in the Eastern Mediterranean.

To me it seems that the only option for the west is to stop supporting 'democracy against dictatorship', because democracy isn't an option any more. The west has to support the dictator Bashar al Assad in order to shoot Iran and Hezbollah in the knees.

Complicated?

Yes.

Can I make my argument plain in a TV programme? And could this result in a rational discussion?

Not really, no. Arab media had its own Arab Spring, some time ago, and Arab leaders utterly fail to recognise that they've no control over social media. In Arab television, I fear we've regressed to a dark age of half-truth, bias and conflict for its own sake.

Chapter 2

A foot in the door

'He who pays the piper calls the tune.' In other words if you own a medium of communication you can dictate how people think. I knew this, in an abstract sort of way, when I got my first degree in Algeria. I'm not sure that the full implications were clear to me, though.

I had studied journalism. As a student, I had obtained an interview with Mayada al Hannawi, a hugely popular Syrian singer, when she visited Algiers. I'd never heard of her, but I found plenty of avid fans among the girl students. Thanks to what they told me, I was able to ask her about a controversial relationship she was in. She gave me honest answers and my article - and the picture of both of us – made the front page of Al Jamhouria, a paper based in Oran. I wrote other pieces after that, and had them published. I was young, enthusiastic, I had proved I could do the job, and I managed to get a first class degree. So I was awarded a bursary to continue my studies abroad.

I wanted to know more about TV. Obviously, I had to go to America. Like every other young Algerian in the late 1980s, for me, television was American - CNN. I'd been watching CNN International programmes since they began in 1985, with Arabic subtitles. BBC World Service TV hadn't yet started and there were no Arab channels at all. CNN programmes didn't reflect our own lives in the least, but they were interesting, and that mattered more.

And most people had TV by then. I'd grown up with the cultural shift that technology brought to North Africa. I'd been a country child, and I remembered a visit to an uncle who had a TV as we did. His wife and daughters sat in the room with us watching a cowboy film. 'They're just *acting*' he said scornfully, as the baddies fell, groaning, in a hail of gunfire and pools of blood. But as the credits rolled, the News was about to come on. The presenter would be looking straight at every woman in this room and who knew what lust might be aroused? Uncle turned and gave my aunt and his daughters a look like thunder, but they were scuttling out to the kitchen already. 'I'm not having that fellah ogling my wife!'

Algeria was catching up now. People were more sophisticated, less deferential after a decade of material poverty. We were all desperate to be better off. I knew that rich people could even buy mobile phones. Who knew what might come next? But America - No, they said. They'd give me a grant to do a Master's and a Doctorate and I'd have a job in the Ministry when I came back, but America? No. Not even Canada. I could go to England.

England? I refused. Calm down, they said; you need to learn English before you can study in America, so go to England first. Then we'll see.

So I set off, with a glum face and hardly a word of English, to learn a new language in an old seaport city in the far south-west of a chilly island. It was excellent. I lived with a family, went to college, and listened and wrote, listened and wrote, and spoke English pretty much all day. Fortunately Plymouth and the Arab world didn't mix much. Apart from me and a few Moroccan students, there was probably one Lebanese family with a kebab shop and an Egyptian cab driver. I had to talk like a local - unless, as occasionally happened, I met a French person. But as I stammered from sentence to sentence, I found English people were patient. That gave me confidence. I started going to the cinema, watching TV, talking to girls - and pretty soon I went from 'getting by' to 'I can do this.' Less than a year after my arrival, I was ready to start a Master's in Mass Communications.

I moved north for that. I did it at Leicester University, up in the Midlands. It was a purely academic course, all about the effects of mass communication on the audience, and how events are selected as news, and who owns the channels. But I needed more money than my bursary could provide so I kept looking for part-time work. The *Guardian*, a national paper, had job advertisements - teachers one day, scientists another, and media people on I think Mondays. One Monday, in Arabic and English, there was a big advertisement for translators, presenters, producers and technicians to work for a new TV company called MBC, in London, which was about to start news broadcasts to the Gulf. This was just what I'd been looking for. I wrote an impressive CV and sent it off, and was invited for an interview.

Off I went, in my smartest suit, to an office in Conduit Street, off Regent Street in central London. I was to meet a Lebanese executive. His secretary, who turned out to be from Hawaii, was charming. Unfortunately she couldn't find my CV. I sat in increasing anxiety while she opened filing cabinets, cupboards, drawers - It turned up at last in a cardboard box labelled JOB APPLICATIONS - UNCLASSIFIED.

The executive was friendly. He read it. 'Ah,' he said. 'You don't specify the position you want. That's why we couldn't find it. So - what have you done?' I told him; my journalism course in Algeria had been quite practical, so I knew how to chase a story, conduct an interview and use a camera – and of course I could translate. That was important, because in Britain a lot of broadcast news originated from Associated Press and Reuters wire services. There was no Arabic wire service. He told me that I'd be called for interview the following week.

Silence. No call for interview. I got a job anyway, part-time at the University. BBC World Service radio broadcasts in Arabic throughout North Africa and the Middle East. They have a rolling program of research into what works, and what doesn't, in places as far apart as Morocco, Somalia and Iraq. In those days field research (answers to questionnaires, in Arabic) from all the different countries were sent to the Centre for Communications at Leicester University for analysis, and I was asked to work there. We'd work out the preferences of a given audience by percentage - '52% of Jordanian respondents think the morning programme over-emphasises news from North Africa,' that sort of thing.

When I started my PhD I had a bursary for the next two years. I was pretty well aware of events back home, and I knew that economy was suffering as the price of oil dropped to $8 a barrel. But in England I felt comparatively unaffected. So I was dismayed when, one day, I received a letter from the Ministry of Education in Algiers. Times were hard. Sorry, they said; we can no longer afford to pay your bursary in the final year of your PhD.

They withdrew the offer of a public service job at the end of it, as well. Now my career trajectory was suspended in mid-air, like a bridge over a ravine.

I had rent to pay and a doctorate to fund, and my pocket money from the BBC analysis didn't remotely cover my living costs. I needed work, so I took anything friends were kind enough to offer. In this way I found myself testing got valuable experience as a counter hand in a kebab shop (you have to keep smiling) and a taxi controller (you have to think quickly despite being practically dead with tiredness after your shift in a kebab shop).

I also worked at the BBC's Monitoring Centre at Caversham, west of London. The BBC has employed native-language listeners to monitor foreign broadcasts since World War II. I enjoyed myself, listening to drama and opinion and news from all the North African radio stations, and reporting on the preferences and attitudes I heard there. Most of these countries had State-run TV, which toed a party line and conveyed pro-régime information, and anodyne entertainment, in classical Arabic. It was rare to hear a dialect speaker and even rarer to hear any kind of controversy.

Arabic-language newspapers and magazines based in London were another small income stream for me. The big news, then, was mostly about Saddam Hussein, but from time to time they needed someone to submit material about Algeria. *Asharq Al Awsat, Al Arab, Al Mjallah* and other papers and periodicals published in London sustained my self-confidence. I was getting experience as a journalist, and my name into print, and to me that was just as important as extra income. Which was a good thing, because they paid very little.

I'd always made it my business to follow news from home by looking at the French papers as well as British and Arabic sources, and I was well aware of underlying violence in the cities back home. I had vivid memories of the time I'd been in Algiers for a brief visit from England in October 1988. I'd seen crowds of unarmed demonstrators pouring out of the Kasbah and other places and converging on the Government offices. Then everybody started running - it seemed the army had confronted the protestors and opened fire at once. It was horrifying. I quickly decided I was too young to die, and looked wildly for a taxi. Nothing. Then I remembered that somebody I knew from Leicester had given me the key to his apartment. I could run there through the back streets, so I did. The racket of gunfire and screaming was awful. I got to the address, let myself in and shut the door behind me. Ten minutes later desperate strangers were trying to get into the building to save themselves from flying bullets.

In the city centre, young people had torn the Algerian flag down and hung up an empty grain-sack. This was the culmination of what they called The Black Decade; they wanted food. The poverty was terrible; the Government had to ask the International Monetary Fund for help but the IMF, who always demand spending cuts, only made life worse. And when they saluted the grain sack - that's when the army started shooting.

5th October, 1988 was really the first Arab spring. Poor people, and students, allied against a brutal military junta, were mown down where they stood. The western media - the French and Americans, at any rate - reported this as a terrorist uprising, which it was not.

A few years had passed since then, and back in England I wrote for Arabic papers, I listened and reported from Caversham, I served the odd kebab, and I kept on working for my PhD. In Algeria the political situation did not improve and nor did the economy.

One day, almost a year after my interview in Conduit Street, I caught sight of a familiar name in an article: MBC, the first ever Arabic TV news channel. The owner was Sheikh Walid al-Ibrahim, a young Saudi brother-in-law of King Fahd, and although the launch had been delayed by the start of the Gulf War, just weeks from now it would start worldwide satellite transmission. It had taken studios in Parson's Green, Fulham, one of the smarter inner suburbs of west London.

It all made sense. Finding the right executives, and arranging a clear guaranteed income stream from the Gulf, must have been a massive undertaking. They'd delayed the launch, so they hadn't taken on any translators. Now, though... I found their phone number and called. An Australian voice answered. I explained that I'd applied a year ago and had been expecting to hear something, but hadn't, and I was still enthusiastic about working for them.

'When can you come in?' he said. 'Are you free tomorrow at ten?'

MBC 1st anniversary in London 1992

I was. I found the MBC studios down a narrow alley off a leafy street. The Australian voice turned out to belong to Stephen Marney, the first Head of News. He explained how MBC had originated six months before my first interview when King Fahd noticed, with irritation, that the only TV channels covering Saddam Hussein's expansionist ambitions were CNN or BBC World. An Iraqi dictator was creeping up to the King's own backyard, and all he could get was a foreigner's eye view. Sheikh Walid was a very smart western-educated young relative who agreed, and knew the solution, so King Fahd backed him in setting up the news channel. It couldn't be based in the Gulf, or it would be accused of bias; and it shouldn't be in the United States, either. London was the obvious compromise. Hundreds of skilled technicians and film-makers were there. British journalists had a good reputation for impartiality. And of course it was in a useful time zone.

Fortunately the British government under John Major was anxious to see inward investment - which created jobs - and had no restrictions on foreign broadcasting stations working out of London.

I'd turned up out of the blue, as a stranger with no TV experience, untested, but eager to join the labour force. The interview seemed to go all right and Stephen introduced me to a member of staff who led me away for a translation test.

I made the translation from English to Arabic and read it aloud in the studio so that my pronunciation could be assessed. That took about an hour. By midday I was out on the sunny street again. 'We'll call you,' I heard. I hoped I wouldn't have to wait another year.

Stephen Marney's secretary rang three hours later. 'Stephen would like you to come in for a three-month probationary period. Are you OK with that?'

YESSSS! 'I would be very happy with it.'

'Great! Can you start working tomorrow?'

I could. A 'probationary' three months was almost certainly an unpaid internship, but I could just afford to support myself and continue studying as long as some paid work came up at the end of it. There was one other issue. I had a place to stay in London, but as I was still studying for a second degree my student visa allowed me to work for only 20 hours a week. I took my papers with me the following morning and explained the situation. They said that was fine, and their lawyers would deal with it for me. So I started work, translating.

The company was about a hundred strong at the time and the senior staff were mainly professional television people, who'd come from the BBC or ITN - which in those days meant most had had BBC training. They'd been editors, producers, directors and administrators for many years. As at the BBC, there was a clear division of labour between money managing on one side, and production of programmes on the other. Producers did of course work to a budget, but the administrators and accountants understood that without a sufficiently generous budget, good programmes could not get made; and without good programmes, none of us would have a job.

All these managers - the ones who looked after the finances as well as the programme-makers - had grown up with the BBC Charter behind them. That was an agreement made in 1927 before TV had been invented, when the BBC (originally a private company) had a monopoly on broadcast radio. The BBC had to get money from somewhere, and the State would be happy to pay for it, but the directors resisted; they understood the implications of being a mouthpiece for government. In the end they negotiated a Royal Charter - a legal agreement, as permanent as the Constitution of a country. The State would collect all the money the BBC needed - a 'licence fee' - from every citizen who could receive broadcasts; and it would not interfere with programme content. Whatever happened, it would not threaten free speech by threatening to withhold money.

The BBC in return would 'inform, educate and entertain'.

Informing, educating and entertaining sound simple but after about a minute and a half of doing them for a mass audience, you realise that you can't choose one way of doing any of those things. If all the information you provide about, say, camel racing, is hostile, the people who love camel racing will switch off. If all you teach them is capitalism, the communists will start forming secret cells. If you only entertain them with Rachmaninov, people will switch to Rai.

And if you don't check every fact, you will be branded a liar.

The principle is clear. You have to be accurate and even-handed, and rise above your own opinion or that of the Government that collects your money and gives it to you.

MBC was funded by Saudi government money. It could have been just another mouthpiece for the owner's opinions, as nearly every State-run broadcaster has proved to be. It had no Charter, no written promise of impartiality.

Yet its senior producers and editors, because they were mostly BBC-trained, insisted on fair-minded programmes, with a voice for every side in an argument, and they expected the same of all the Arab programme-makers and presenters who worked there. These employees were women as well as men and most came with experience from the media in their own country, either in the Middle East or North Africa. Often they'd worked at newspapers, since jobs in TV at home were hard to find. There was a predominance of Lebanese and Syrian presenters. I liked working at MBC because after several years of having few Arab friends, I soon had many.

I enjoyed translating for TV, and was learning something, because I got the opportunity to produce short pieces for news bulletins that went out for five minutes in every hour. We'd often get agency footage that came complete with ambient sound and British or American voice-over; I'd have to replace the English with an Arabic commentary. English is brisk, while Arabic is florid. You can say things in two words in English where Arabic takes six, and when you're trying to match words to pictures, that doesn't make the task easy. The news editor, a Brit, had thirty minutes in which to tell stories from each of the 22 countries our Pan-Arab channel was covering, plus international news. Our audience were Arabs of numerous diasporas, and items of Arab interest might come in from Paris or Buenos Aires. If we rarely covered them there would be complaints.

There were three main news broadcasts a day, at 3pm, 6pm and 9pm British time; the editor would therefore select his daily running order weighing political importance, social impact and interesting footage in the balance - and each news might have slightly different stories about the same item, or entirely different items. And as if that wasn't difficult enough, he would be dealing with the unconscious bias of all the producers. Some wanted to cover stories that would confirm their own prejudices, some wanted only the good side of their own country to appear, and others wanted conflict, conflict, conflict - the bloodier the better - to make gripping TV.

The editor would end up with, say, seven stories of which the final one would be light-hearted. If a producer failed to get his own item off the ground he would spend his day making an item we could archive - something that was interesting, but not newsworthy, which we could show any time in the next couple of weeks or months.

Let's say I had to produce a news item about the death of a beloved Algerian singer. 'I can give you one minute thirty, max' the editor would say. We'd have stock footage of the singer - whose performance must be heard of course - and a clip from a TV interview with her; and general views of grieving people outside the house where she had lived and died - which was almost the only part I could cover with voice-over about her fan base, her best-known songs, her age at death, where she died, that sort of thing. A suitably respectful voice-over in Arabic would take 50 seconds, which would leave no time for the song or the interview clip. I'd have to cut it down to 20 seconds.

We had to develop a terse, immediate style in Arabic.

Also we'd be sent footage with sound but no voice-over, just a short identifier. I thought I had to fit commentary to footage, so at first that's what I did. The videotape editor didn't say anything. Stuart, the most senior news editor, watched the results with me.

'What's happening here?' he asked, as my voice in Arabic explained the pictures on the screen.

'They're shooting at the police and that guy's shouting about the Governor.'

'Yes, but it's video, right? Pictures and sound. You've drowned out the soundtrack and you're telling us what we know. I can see they're shooting. I can see the guy's agitated. Why don't you let the pictures and sound tell the story?'

'Ah.'

I got it. It wasn't radio. The action mattered most. The brain takes in visual information immediately. And if you have to talk over the pictures - as sometimes you do - pictures and sound must cohere. Otherwise it's like watching a man in a Mickey Mouse costume reading the news; there's a mismatch, and you can't concentrate on either the picture or the sound.

I learned fast because I wanted to keep this job. I loved it, and - more importantly - I needed it; without the practical experience I was getting, my doctorate (when I got it) would not count for so much in getting a full-time job in television. Preferably I wanted to stay in Europe, because seen from here, life in Algeria was getting more violent with every week that passed.

MBC attracted a big audience almost at once. Ordinary people, not multilingual intellectuals who were always glued to CNN, gravitated towards our station because we broadcast in Arabic and our news was slanted towards matters of interest to them. We were not afraid to use demotic Arabic and have people talk in local dialect, and we didn't act as a PR company for any of the régimes but did our best to find the truth among competing accounts of what was going on. Our tagline was *The World Through Arab Eyes.*

Later we would have correspondents in every key capital city but at first MBC was represented only in Washington, Jerusalem and Cairo. Jerusalem was a master-stroke, because for the first time ordinary Arabs could see the Israeli flag, the Israeli Prime Minister and the Knesset. The Madrid Conference on the Palestinian/Israeli conflict began a the end of October,

'91, and MBC sent a big team. Netanyahu, who was Foreign Minister then, gave us an interview. He spoke in English but he knew he was addressing an Arab audience.

Towards the end of my three month probationary period an American-educated Saudi was introduced to the company. He would be Director General, one management step above Stephen. Stephen was happy with my attitude and the work I was doing, but this new guy never said a word to me. He'd come into the newsroom and speak only to editors.

One day I translated a report on heightened tensions in Kashmir, and put the pictures together. It was used in the important 6pm edition of the News, and the footage was marvellous: aerial shots, from a helicopter, of majestic mountain ranges and green valleys. It did wonders for the report, I thought.

I was in the newsroom working towards the 9pm bulletin when the Director General came in. A woman from New Zealand, a producer, was sitting next to me. He came over and spoke to me in Arabic. 'That's what we want. That's the style. Come and see me tomorrow to get your contract.' He looked at my neighbour. 'Did you understand?' he said, in English. 'I know a compliment when I hear one,' she smiled.

I had my big break. What a relief. I signed up as a producer and translator and they began the process of obtaining a work permit for me. Until then, I hadn't done anything about getting paid; internships in television are often unpaid and I never gave it a thought. But one of the admin people stopped me in a corridor - 'Did you know you've got some money waiting for you?' she said. 'We've been keeping it. There are three cheques.'

I had money and something to celebrate, and my future seemed assured. I was full of enthusiasm and confidence.

Chapter 3

Promotion, kind of

'Have a look at this.'

Stuart Young, the news editor, was at my desk. He had a press release, in English and Arabic, about a conference of Arab poets that was to take place at the Arab Writers' Club in Queensway. Nizar Qabbani would be there.

'There's a story in it. D'you think you can do it? You'll have to get over there now and do a couple of interviews and a piece to camera. I want it for the six o'clock.'

'I'll go,' I said.

'OK, take Raef and Lee with you.' We had two in-house crews at the time, one a Palestinian cameraman with an Englishman to do the sound, and the other where the cameraman was Lebanese and the soundman was Danish. 'I want two minutes.'

I said a silent prayer of thanks for my crew, Raef Debaja and Lee Weller, because I'd never been on a shoot before. All I could do was watch what they did, get the story as I usually would, and say something to the camera. I combed my hair and straightened my tie, helped them to pile their heavy aluminium cases of equipment into the boot of the car, and we set off for Queensway. 'Right,' Raef said on the way. 'I've got lights, because we'll be indoors, so I'll set up and you can bring the Famous Poets over for their interviews. And I'll do the establishing shots when we leave. Where is this place?'

It was an old public library with a stone exterior and - fortunately for the pictures - a lot of bookshelves that would make an appropriate background. I helped offload the equipment, which even on a simple shoot was a whole lot bulkier than it is now with a monitor, amplifier, and yards of cable in all the boxes. I then met the poets while Raef and Lee set up.

This was a small and relatively leisurely shoot but the two professionals worked together like clockwork. It took them less than ten minutes to link all the cables and position the lights, and we were ready to go.

I'd expected to feel self-conscious but I didn't, because it was clear to me that my tiny crew couldn't care less what I was actually saying; and that this would always be the case. What the talent (as the crew ironically name anyone who's being filmed, whether it's Robert de Niro or the dumbest reporter) does is of very little significance, as long as they do it in the right place. The sound man, who is wearing headphones, is absorbed in watching oscillating needles so that the volume doesn't cross a red line and start to distort; often he's simultaneously balancing a big mic on the end of a pole just high enough above a speaker's head to be out of shot. For the cameraman you might as well be a pot plant. His job is to produce brilliantly framed, properly exposed, beautifully focussed pictures of Mr PotPlant and all the others. These people have been doing their jobs for so long that they react to action and excitement with abstraction. They don't need to be told when to zoom in, or to use a particular kind of microphone; and cameramen have an amazing awareness of what's happening just out of range, so that the good ones can pull out to a wide shot to catch whatever it is. They sense events beyond the viewfinder.

I learned something, without even thinking about it. The correspondent and crew were interdependent. None of us could work without the others. Real friendships develop in television for that reason. It's like being an actor in a play or a soldier in a platoon.

The writers were a friendly bunch. There were Iraqis and Egyptians but the most famous person there was Nizar Qabbani, from Damascus, who had lived in London for nearly a decade then. He was unusual in having a distinguished hinterland: he'd been a diplomat. Everyone of my generation knew his poetry. Much of it was romantic, erotic – and the heartbreak of his life was well known. His older sister had committed suicide rather than marry a man she did not love, and his second wife Balqis died when the Iraqi Embassy in Beirut was bombed in 1981. In his poem *Balqis* he had expressed not only grief, but fury at the conceited, self-importantly aggressive Arab culture that he blamed for her death. He fiercely opposed any dismissive treatment of women, and he loathed trigger-happy reactions to challenge.

In London he saw that liberty was a double-edged sword: yes, we were all free to say and do what we want, but these rights extended to the international super-rich who lived here and could use their money to influence the media. 'The camel-rider buys Fleet Street,' one of his poems was called. A beautiful old man.

with the famous Poet Nizar Qabbani at the Arab Press Club in lonfon 1993

Most of these writers freely said that they would love to go home but life in the Middle East was restrictive and dangerous. They were charming, urbane interviewees with something interesting to say.

In my life, I have interviewed some ill-disciplined, surly people. But this time, good fortune was following me. Back at the studios I cut the report together. It was a good interview, and it went out on the 6pm news. Later that evening, Stuart came in just as I was about to leave the newsroom.

'That's it,' he said, smiling. 'Hacene, this is your last day as producer. You're an MBC correspondent from now on.'

'Really?'

'Really. Come and see me in the morning. You'll need a new contract and a press card.'

I went home on the Tube grinning from ear to ear.

The next day he told me what I'd be expected to do. Every day I'd find a British story, usually one with an Arab angle. I'd put it before the editor at the morning editorial meeting, and if he accepted it I'd take a crew out and do it. When I came back with the footage, I'd be told how long the piece had to be, and I'd cut it to that length. Of course, by that time it could have been shelved altogether because something more important had arisen - News moves very, very fast, and our huge international audience were nearly all interested in their own domestic politics above than anything else.

Fortunately I had learned in my first few months exactly how quick TV reportage is. I could never have just walked into this job. I'd needed to see how a TV station worked, and make short bulletins for myself, and understand the importance of timing by getting it right at work every day.

When visitors came from the Middle East, we would take them to our darkened viewing gallery above the control desk. They'd see the double bank of television screens below and watch the countdown before the News. Different things were happening on all the screens. On set, two brightly-lit presenters would be watching the clock. The director, with an editor at his side, would be at the mixing desk with his running order in front of him. They would see the titles roll up, hear the signature music play, and watch the editor fading recorded sound down and studio voices up and mixing from title sequence to set. News announcements would begin, with film under voice-over cutting to studio shots from each of three cameras - 'Go to camera three' - 'Graphic' – They'd watch the director cutting back and forth, instructing a cameramen occasionally: 'Zoom in camera 2' if a studio interviewee was particularly emotional - They'd see concentrated co-ordination of sound, vision and frame-perfect timing for half an hour. They'd watch the recorded news items being introduced and the presenters signing off at the end, while the director was saying-

' – Fifteen seconds... ten... five' - and the hand on the mixing desk would bring the final music up and the credits would roll across the screen.

We all knew our jobs. We had all learned those techniques. The precision and rapidity of it shocked our visitors every time. Some of these guys never did anything time-delimited in daily life. In fact some of them rarely caught a scheduled flight.

My easiest assignments were in London. The King of Jordan lived here, and if we wanted his opinion we called the Embassy's press department and he usually obliged. Sometimes there was a comment worth recording from the Saudi Ambassador, or an official visit by Saudi royalty, and when the Israeli Prime Minister was in London I got an interview with him, too.

As a news channel, we went from strength to strength throughout in the next couple of years. I worked on many assignments outside Britain, including Bill Clinton's election campaign in 1992 and his address to the US troops in Kuwait City 1994.

MBC made a point of covering Arab communities of the distant diaspora. Most Arabs in the Middle East and North Africa were barely aware that there were others, just like them, on every continent. North Africans like me, often rural people, usually emigrate to Europe, while city-dwellers from the eastern Mediterranean go to the Americas, north and south.

We were, though, a news channel, and it was hardly news that these thriving communities existed, so we tended to hang our human-interest items around a central news story. When a Jewish community centre in

Buenos Aires was devastated by a bomb in '94 I went there to make a piece about the Arabs of Argentina. Iran and Hezbollah were apparently behind the terrorism but the people in the Arab community were angry that a violent minority had indirectly made people suspicious of them. They had integrated well into Argentinian society up to now.

The Saudi ambassador had suggested the documentary to MBC so they went there and I made a two-parter called *Forgotten People:* the Arabs of Argentina. Not that they were forgotten in Argentina itself – Carlos Menem was the President and his family had come originally from Syria, so he gave us an interview. And I met a lot of people who identified themselves as Arabs but had been born in Argentina and spoke only Spanish (fade up the Tango and watch the dancing in the streets....) They had what they wanted: halal butchers, mosques, and a strong business community. Admittedly, the Moslem burial grounds were full and the City wouldn't let them buy any more land. But 'forgotten' – only by the media back home. In South America, they were integrated.

As for the Saudi Ambassador, he owned about 6,000 acres of grazing land in Argentina. There he raised lambs which were destined for Mecca, to feed the hundreds of thousands who arrived for the Haj every year.

I have visited numerous diaspora communities. Here are some generalisations - and that's all they are - based on what I have seen.

I conclude that first-generation arrivals from the eastern Mediterranean usually succeed, not only because they participate in the life of the indigenous community, but because they nurture a support network amongst themselves. If people from north Africa tend not to form such networks, it's probably because they're not city-dwellers with a background in trade. Business people are nothing without contacts they can trust. In cities, Maghrebis look for employers rather than people to trade with or sell to. Of the millions in France, a great many are employed in industry. They rely on regular employment rather than entrepreneurship, so the community of people from their own background is not so important.

Why one set of people succeeds in business, and another doesn't, is of interest to me. I was educated in North Africa, happy with my parents and my extended family, but there was no endeavour there that seemed worth staying for. And since then, the régimes have done nothing to create a climate in which business can flourish. Palestinians feel much the same. They'd like to go home, but they've moved to America or Britain, lands of opportunity, and there's nothing comparable in Palestine.

If you voice this thought in North Africa or the Middle East, as Edward Saïd did, you're perceived as a traitor, a threat. 'He's lived in the west so he's out to get us.' Fortunately the régimes are dropping like confetti, and the tide of history is against them.

Chapter 4

Calling card

interviewing British Prime Minister John Major during the
inauguration ceremony of MBC Studios in Battersea 1994

MBC moved in 1993 to bigger, better-equipped studios in Battersea, across
the river from Chelsea in south London, opposite a park. John Major came
to cut the ribbon and declare it open. By then there were already 400
people working at our London HQ and we had correspondents in the key
capitals of the world.

This was a bright moment but the United Kingdom was in the doldrums.
Civil war in Northern Ireland was an ongoing problem and nobody seemed

to know how to improve the economy, which bumped along at the bottom unable to rise.

A couple of years before, inflation had been rapid and interest rates soaring, but both had come down before starting to rise again, and John Major's government had joined the ERM - the Exchange Rate Mechanism. ERM membership was supposed to be a transition phase before the Euro became our new currency. It would be adopted by most countries of the European Union, Britain included.

It didn't work out like that. Britain couldn't keep up, economically, with Germany and was forced to make a humiliating departure from the ERM. This proved (in the end) to be a good thing, but nobody knew that at the time. The Chancellor, Norman Lamont, was about the most unpopular fellow in Britain. Yet the same people kept getting voted back into power, because most voters were even more suspicious of the opposition. There was plenty to say, most of it none too flattering, and I covered many Party Conferences and reports on the decline of British industry.

And then there was Northern Ireland. There is too much history behind the ongoing dispute in Northern Ireland to go into here - the Catholics still resented the Protestant victory of three hundred years before, so I won't start - but hatred resulted in a terrorist bombing campaign in Northern Ireland and Britain. It had been going on since the late 1960s but in my first year with MBC there were huge explosions in the City and Canary Wharf, which are the old and new sections of the financial district.

The most dangerous hotel in Europe was the Europa in Belfast, the capital of Northern Ireland. The world's media spoke from the Europa and it had been bombed many times, once in 1993 so badly as to be require major rebuilding. Anyhow, I stayed there like every other TV journalist. There was usually trouble in the Marching Season. This was the time - around April - when the Protestants, waving orange banners, and walking with noisy pipe bands, deliberately marched through the Catholic streets in cities all over Northern Ireland inviting retaliation. The British Army was usually in close attendance but civilians got killed all the time.

On the occasions when I was there they didn't, despite gunfire; although I do remember cowering behind a tank, once, dodging fire with Kate Adie.

'Bet you'd rather be in Tiananmen Square,' I muttered. She laughed. She was famous for her fearless broadcasts from there at the height of the aborted uprising in '91.

I came back to London rather pleased with myself. Belfast was a trouble-spot, but I'd come back safely: I knew my job. At least I thought so.

So when you're young and confident and somebody from work calls you at home at 10 o'clock at night and says

'Look, this is crucial. There's been a policy decision. Can you go to North Yemen in the morning?'

– you say 'Yes,' without thinking, don't you? Well, I did.

I don't think the person had expected this, because there was a pause. Then he said quietly

'Are you *sure?*'

Of course I was sure. This was just another assignment, albeit more dangerous.

I set off early the next day. I had an experienced crew. They would at least save me from making a fool of myself. The cameraman was a Brit, Nick Ludlow, and the sound recordist was Abed, a Lebanese who had worked with CNN.

It was the spring of 1994. Yemen had been in the news a lot, so I knew the background to the war we were going to. For many years the country had been officially divided into North and South Yemen. The northern tribes - who numbered tens of millions, and had a porous border with Saudi Arabia – and the much smaller population of socialist south Yemen, got on well enough, most of the time.

They'd finally united (not for the first time) as one country in 1990. Between them they'd cooked up at least the appearance of a democratic constitution. Sana'a (in the north) would be the seat of government and Aden (in the south) the economic engine. At the time, both sides had newly-discovered reserves of oil and gas. The south, having lost Russian aid with the break-up of the Soviet Union, was only too happy to be part of a bigger country. The North's motive in pushing for union was obscure, but it became clearer once unity was achieved. Thanks to President Saleh the British-trained, Russia-supplied Yemeni army in the north quietly came to control all the key strategic points in the country.

The new Yemen was socialist with Ba'athist sympathies, and so was Saleh, so when in 1991 Saddam Hussein invaded Kuwait, the government of Yemen refused to speak or act against him. The unexpected consequence was that King Fahd of Saudi Arabia deported nearly a million Yemeni workers from his country. They came back to refugee camps in the north. The country as a whole suffered from losing the money they'd previously sent to their families, and there was no work for them at home. There were food riots, and a minority party of northern Islamist fighters stirred up even more trouble.

By 1992 the north and south were arguing and in '93 war broke out. The south had trusted that unity was permanent, but it wasn't. The north had the seat of government, the army, a big arsenal of old Russian arms, some territory, some Islamist guerrillas and by far the larger number of people. They were well prepared and the President, in the north, had strong tribal links. The south was secular, with a rebel army, a key port, and the ever-present threat of air attack from Eritrea or Djibouti. Rather late in the day - because they'd trusted Saleh - they got help from Saudi Arabia and the United States.

MBC London sent a crew with Toufiq Gazoulit, my Moroccan colleague, to report from Aden, in the south. There were problems with this. Positioned as he was behind a battle line, Toufiq could not reflect opinion in the north. There were rumblings of complaint in the newsroom. Our coverage was biased in favour of the Saudi, western point of view - literally and metaphorically.

We must maintain our core ethos, which had always been impartiality. That was the 'policy decision'. The station must send some reckless fool to the North as well. So off I went.

❖

We planned to change planes in Cairo, but we landed only to find that flights to Sana'a had been cancelled. We called MBC's local office and they spoke to the Yemeni Embassy. We were in luck. Yemen's Foreign Minister, Mohamed Basindawa, was visiting Cairo as part of a whistle-stop tour of the middle east. He was returning early tomorrow via Amman, in a private plane, and would give us a lift.

Fine. All we had to was get a good night's sleep at an airport hotel. Nick was an old hand at filming in dangerous places, so I hoped to learn what I could from him when we had a drink before dinner. He was leaning on the bar with a glass of whisky in his hand.

'Mind if I ask you Hacene...Is this your first go at a shooting war?'

'Except for Northern Ireland, yes.'

'OK,' he said 'Then I think we should play it my way. I promise you that I will make you the best war correspondent in the Arab world. But you have to trust me.'

'I'll do whatever it takes.'

'That's good. We'll all be safer. What are you drinking?'

That evening he told me the Key Points.

'Rule number one: it's not your quarrel. You are not part of it. You are not interested in dying in it.'

'Very true.'

'Rule number two: *hurry up*. When we're filming in a war zone we're fast. It minimises risk. We don't hang about. You wanna get it done in less than an hour, and go.'

'An hour?'

'OK, ninety minutes if you have to. But this is *not* about being perfect. It's about being alive. Take direction from me and I'll position you to the camera.'

'All right.'

I must have looked nervous because he said kindly 'It's not all dangerous. War isn't just about Bang Bang You're Dead. It's what it does to individuals that matters. If I see a human interest angle you haven't noticed I'll mention it.'

Basindawa, a small, balding fellow, worked on his papers on the plane, but he had a few words for us. He was keen to keep the country together by finding an amicable solution, he told us, and promised that when we'd reached our destination and got accreditation, he would give us an interview.

We stopped in Amman for several hours and he was driven away for talks. I was impatient to get to Sana'a. Nothing seemed more important than getting film back to London. MBC badly wanted something, no matter what, as long as it showed us reporting from North Yemen.

At last a limousine conveyed Basindawa back, and we all set off. When we arrived at Sana'a we had to wait again at the airport while they found a government technician called Hamoud to examine the video equipment.

A taxi took us to the hotel. Market stalls and shops were open, and the streets were thronged with people, a lot of them buzzing about on scooters. There was a military presence, but it wasn't overwhelming.

Old Sana'a is as exotic as it looks in photographs: a vast huddle of tall, ornate sand coloured buildings, picked out in pale filigree, lining steep alleyways buzzing with life. As soon as we got there, we decided to put our stuff in the hotel and go out at once. I wanted to get a report back fast because we'd been delayed by a day already. Sitting about in a Government office while accreditation was arranged could be delayed until tomorrow.

Having no better ideas yet, we began with GVs - general views, the sort of street-scene cliché that's invaluable for showing where you are; red London buses, yellow New York taxis, or in this case the narrow, crowded alleys and unmistakeable mediaeval high-rises of Sana'a. We happened to stop quite close to some people sleeping on the ground. Nick had fixed the camera onto the tripod and was peering through the lens, twiddling knobs. Abed had squatted on the ground to open a case and I was making a note on a pad. I looked up and saw that we were surrounded by half a dozen armed soldiers. Their officer looked annoyed..

'What d'you think you're doing?'

'Working. We're from MBC TV in London.'

'Give me your papers. Why are you taking pictures of these people?'

'We're looking at the whole street, not just them. We left our papers in our hotel.'

'Which hotel?'

I gave the name. 'We only got here half an hour ago. Mohamed Basindawa gave us seats in his plane from Cairo because flights are cancelled.'

He looked shocked. 'So why are you filming beggars? You're making propaganda.'

'No we're not.'

'Tell him to give me the film.'

I told Nick. 'He wants the tape. Have you...'

'No - there's nothing on it.' Nick removed the tape from the machine. 'I haven't even switched on.'

I told the officer 'We're just here to do a job. We're not making propaganda. We're not interested in your politics. The tape's empty.'

'So you say. I'm going to watch it myself,' he said, grim-faced as Nick handed him the tape. 'You're coming with us.'

'If you don't find anything will you apologise and let us carry on?'

'We'll see.'

We were led around a corner and into a big 4-wheel drive with two of the soldiers and the commander. They drove us to a building which, according to a sign outside, was the central office of the General Congress Party – Saleh's party. I was relieved, because this reassured me that we weren't about to be interrogated or detained. We crowded into a small editing suite, with monitors. A familiar face appeared: Hamoud.

The tape was empty, of course. And Hamoud confirmed that we'd arrived only hours before in Mohammed Basindawi's plane. The atmosphere warmed up a bit, but the officer was still suspicious. I had to get him on our side. Our ability to transmit depended on the goodwill of Yemeni State TV and I didn't want intervention from on high.

I decided our arrest had been a shot across the bows; a way to show they were in control. I said

'I'm sorry we didn't fix up the accreditation first. We put it off 'til tomorrow because MBC is in a big hurry to have a report to show that we're here.'

'A report biased against our government.'

'Not at all. We're open to ideas. What do you want us to show? A press conference? we'll cover it. We'll be happy to interview the President. All I've got to do is get what I can - two reports a day, even – they won't mind.'

'We want you to show what the people of Yemen really think!'

'Then allow us to ask them. Let us go out in Sana'a and in the villages and interview people. MBC will show it all.'

He hesitated. 'Wait,' he said. 'I want to speak to somebody.'

When he came back, everything went smoothly. Accreditation was issued and we were on the street and filming within an hour. That night, the 6pm news was headlined 'MBC in Sana'a.' The report showed the City's military presence and some vox pops with passers-by. People said they wanted Yemen to stay united, and that the rebels down south were separatists, supported by Gulf money. I did a piece to camera from a steep hill with the labyrinthine Old City behind me. There was a report from Aden as well, and that became the pattern for the whole time we were there. MBC showed both sides of the conflict every night.

The following day we made another short item and attended the President's press conference. Basindawa was on the podium with him, as was the Vice-President, notorious for his strong dislike of anything related to the Gulf states. A lot of foreign media were there; we'd seen a few of them at our hotel but here there were others. The President issued a withering attack an the south's Saudi backers and a triumphant account of the north's advance, and asked for questions. I put my hand up at once.

'Hacene Zitouni MBC London. This war is hurting the ordinary people in Yemen, so how long do you expect it to continue?'

He glowered at me. 'It would be over a lot sooner if your Saudi television station stopped broadcasting lies from Aden. MBC represents a bunch of reactionary separatists and you have the nerve to come here and ask me this? Consider yourself lucky to be alive. If the *ordinary people* of Sana'a knew you were here they'd kill you.'

'Excuse me, Mr President, but we have been filming here and the people of Sana'a have welcomed us. They offered us fruit. We find we have a lot in common. I'm Algerian, and many of the words you use in Yemen are the ones I'm used to hearing at home. I have found nothing but courtesy and kindness.'

'If you think of yourself as some kind of goodwill ambassador,' growled the Vice-President 'you should be ashamed to work for MBC. What is it, d'you need the money?'

'I'm proud to work for MBC sir. It's a station that tries to show all sides of the question, which is why we have a correspondent here as well as one in Aden.'

Arabic speakers in the audience came up to me afterwards. 'You didn't give an inch. Good for you,' muttered one of them. 'One of them tried put the frighteners on and the other one tried to humiliate you. Typical bullying tactics.'

We'd filmed the whole transaction and transmitted it to MBC. It went out as the daily report from Sana'a and included clips of the President's attack on the Saudis and the Gulf states.

The following day Foreign Minister Basindawa, a more diplomatic fellow, gave us a conciliatory interview. He explained although Yemen had refused to support the American incursion into Iraq, President Saleh had never been a supporter of Saddam Hussein. He had merely opposed any western presence in the Gulf. The Gulf war was over now, and Yemen would happily collaborate with Kuwait and the rest. I suggested that the Vice-President might not be happy to do that.

'He has legitimate concerns, of course.' That was all I could get out of him.

I'd been told that the Vice-President had a chip on his shoulder because generations ago, the family of Ibn Saud had somehow managed to claim oil rights that should have belonged to Yemenis. Tribal leaders had sold them, and he thought they'd been cheated.

We rented a vehicle and went out to film in the villages. People here were barely touched by the bombing in the cities. Most scraped by in the same way that they'd been doing for thousands of years, with water from the well, camels and goats, and reliable crops of pistachios and dates. Some cash was coming in. In remote villages, where dried-mud houses huddled up dried-mud lanes worn by generations of people and animals, you'd see a moped owned by the son who'd gone to work in town, or a motorised flatbed tricycle battered from years of service. On flat roofs you'd see bright green plastic buckets from China and plastic sacks of Cuban sugar from Russia.

I saw generators, cables and antennae as well in some villages and I was astonished to be recognised by name. MBC was only three years old, but even these people were watching it. I'd known of course that MBC had an international reach, but somehow I'd imagined only city folk watched us. That wasn't true at all. The men in these villages probably got into town once a month and the women almost never, but they watched MBC from London at home. Its news gave a panoramic view of world affairs, unlike the parochial tub-thumping of State television, and most importantly, it was in Arabic.

That was what so annoyed people like Saleh, right down to the officer who had taken us in for questioning. If the BBC or any of the international networks said someone like Saleh was a dictator, they'd say it in English or French. They'd transmit with sub-titles in countries with poor literacy, or with a voice-over translation that stepped delicately around sensitive words. There'd be no reaction from government. But we spoke directly to the audience in their own language, and that scared the regimes.

In the more primitive villages I wondered how on earth Saleh could justify war when there was so much to do. Education, health care, sanitation... As we got to higher, wetter land further into the tribal territory of the north there was more evidence of a comfortable life. Some of the mediaeval hill towns were as spectacular as Sana'a but tourists were unknown. Qat was being grown on high terraces. I don't know if it was exported much, but the domestic market for qat seemed insatiable It was currency: a reliable way of getting things done. Lavish bundles of the stuff were displayed on market stalls along with baskets of nuts and seeds. We quickly learned that if we bought some, had dinner with some soldiers and gave them qat afterwards, they'd agree to drive us out to the villages.

We'd asked from the start to go to the front line, but had met with cold rejection. That changed after a few days. MBC was now broadcasting, nightly, the views of 'ordinary people' all over north Yemen as well as the south, and somebody important must have been getting positive feedback because the regime's attitude changed.

Either that or they judged that – in the famous words of former US President Lyndon B Johnson - they'd rather have us inside the tent pissing out, than outside the tent pissing in.

So we signed a Government disclaimer form and set off towards the action, along with a multinational crew of other journalists - print, radio, TV – who'd been asking for permission to go there and threatening to leave if they didn't get it. Most of us had been in Sana'a for at least a week and knew one another by sight. As we gathered, fully equipped with cameras and the hulking satphones we had then, to pile into one of four ancient military helicopters, I noticed for the first time that I didn't look quite like the other war correspondents. I suddenly felt weedy. They all seemed to be bulkier, even the women.

There was a reason for this. The big networks issued their correspondents with bullet-proof vests. Further, the BBC, Reuters and the rest routinely paid for people like John Simpson and Martin Bell, and their crews, to learn how to behave if they were taken hostage, injured or kidnapped. Before they got on that helicopter, these people knew about observation, first aid, checking for booby traps, how to cross a minefield and how to rescue someone from a battlefield. BBC News had its own Risk Control Manager and correspondents weren't allowed to report from a war zone unless they'd done at least one course run by ex-Commandos on a country estate outside London, with sniper bullets flying and car-bombs going off unexpectedly. They also took courses in nuclear, biological and chemical weapons protection and later on I found out that the BBC had a couple of armoured vehicles for use in the field.

Even freelances paid for their own courses in kidnap survival, run by ex-military security operatives. It reduced their insurance payments.

MBC? None of that. Not that they wanted us to die, but presumably they trusted in the will of Allah. As for insurance, it had no place in the world of our employer. Insurance was an irrelevance to the Saudi royals. The whole point of it is to remove worry about accidents leading to 'something you can't pay for'. Afloat on an ocean of money, King Fahd could pay for anything. I had to trust my employers to shoulder the responsibility if I or my family required assistance. It is a paternalistic system, open to abuse, but as long as the Saudis remain stupendously wealthy and benevolent towards their employees, it will work.

in Yemen covering the North-South War

So while the other correspondents had been issued with flak jackets that looked like puffed-out photographer's jackets, I climbed into the helicopter wearing a real, loosely flapping photographer's jacket, with plenty of pockets, and struggling with a satphone heavy enough to give me a hernia. I found a place to sit, lit a cigarette and hoped for the best. A big metal cube stood, inert and inexplicable, in the middle of all of us. It puzzled me, but nobody else seemed curious and I didn't want to display my ignorance so I tried to ignore it.

At last I heard an American say

'What the hell's that thing?'

We all looked at it. Silence. Then

'It is the fuel tank,' said a Frenchman.

'Oh.'

About eight of us stubbed out cigarettes in unison.

To distract myself from the tank, I tried to remember Nick's instructions of the night before.

'I want to say something,' he'd said. 'You're doing good reports but you're too much of a perfectionist.' Too slow, he meant. I'd listened, but only now, as I sat uneasily next to the most combustible item in the plane, did the point come home to me. I tried to recall the details. 'Identify one issue. Get the pictures fast. Get the interview fast. Get your piece to camera in the can. And it's job done, outta there. You've shown MBC you're on top of it.' I resolved to work with record-breaking speed.

We flew over over dark volcanic mountains and hundreds of miles of rocky, sandy scrubland, until we came close to Taiz, a hilltop city in the far south-west approached by precipitous mountain roads. Down there the market stalls would be piled high with local grapes and pomegranates and bananas. People would be going about their business. Trade in places like Sana'a, Taiz and Hadramut stopped for nothing. But on the surrounding plain, we could see flashes and smoke from shelling. The north had driven the southerners right back, and we landed just behind the front line. We could hear gunfire but and see the opposing forces only from on high, so we took the equipment up a hillside and set up to make our report with fighting in the distance behind me. I was talking to camera when a big shell shot past - I dived - and it landed with an enormous THUD and flying stones.

It was over. I raised my head and looked for Nick and Abed. Nick wasn't there.

'Gotcha!' he said, grinning from behind the camera. He hadn't flinched. When I saw the pictures I was amazed. He'd filmed everyone, soldiers, and all the correspondents diving to the ground under a hail of rocks. They were terrific pictures. A cameraman like that makes a story come alive. As for me, after that I worked even faster.

Sending our reports to London was a primitive operation twenty years ago. It wasn't live, for a start, unless you were in Sana'a using the satellite connection from the state's TV studios. Sana'a was not much more than an hour's flight away and we had to go back there to edit our footage. At the front line I had a satphone with which I could tell the story, in audio only, and as MBC transmitted 24 hours a day I could take advantage of times when they weren't putting out key bulletins - around midday in Yemen, around 8am in London - to describe what was going on. London could record my call to use as voice-over.

One night CNN called. They wanted to do a daily interview by telephone, with me, and use MBC's coverage from the north because they couldn't get their own crew into Sana'a. I checked with London and was told that would be fine. CNN didn't pay me, but they gave MBC a credit.

The shelling got heavier, and we had to hide in trenches. I climbed down next to a skinny young soldier with an old Kalashnikov, absorbed in prising a tough strand of qat from of his teeth with a fingernail. He stopped.

'I've seen you,' he said. 'You're on MBC.'

'Yup.'

43

'Why did they send *you*?'

'Who'd you want them to send?'

'Well, Nicole, or Kalthoum, or Kawthar...'

He'd named the three best-known women presenters on the channel. I wasn't exactly flattered, but I was over-awed at the recognition. It was all one world.

The northerners had already got possession of the old military bases around Taiz; the separatists couldn't hold them. But even the official Yemeni army - originally trained by Brits, and later supplied with arms by Russians – were not as effective on the ground as the Islamist contingent. This wasn't just because the Islamists were motivated by religious fervour. They were better equipped.

I can't remember whether or not I pointed this out in a broadcast - I probably didn't - but I certainly didn't withhold the truth, which was that the northerners were gaining ground quickly. The London controller of news was now a Syrian, the former editor of a Saudi newspaper published in London. He started calling me.

'You know,' he said 'you're not giving us a true picture, here. They're lying to you.'

'Who's lying? I'm in the thick of it all day. I can see what's going on.'

'The Army's giving you these pictures.'

'Rubbish. Nick Ludlow's filmed every frame I've sent you.'

'I'm sorry, but I can't think we're getting an accurate account here.'

'Listen. I'm telling you the truth. I wouldn't risk my life for anything less. We were less than twenty miles from Aden this morning. And if you don't like the truth the best thing I can do is pack my bags and come back on the next plane. With the crew.'

Impasse.

I thought about it and decide to appeal to someone whose ideas about impartial reporting had been learned in the west. I rang the Saudi Director General and explained that I was under pressure. I'd been getting similar calls from the Syrian controller just about every night.

'I know you trust him, but I'm news reporter, not a politician, and we film what we see. If he doesn't like it I'd rather leave here than tell a load of lies. Is that what he's trying to make me do?'

'No, ' he said. 'Don't leave. We're very pleased with your work. I'll have a word with him. You are implementing a change in policy. MBC's back on the track it should be on. Unbiased reporting is what we want. Maybe that's a difficult for people to grasp at first. I'll sort it out.'

That worked. I got no more trouble from home. Sometimes MBC ran my reports first, sometimes Toufiq's from Aden, but always with a wipe from one piece to the next so that the viewer knew we were getting two sides of the story. I was approached by a Sana'a newspaper; I mentioned it to the London office, and they told me to go ahead and give them the interview they wanted.

I met the guy over tea in the hotel foyer. How did I see the situation here? This was their conflict, I said, not mine, so I could only tell him that I was getting a generally positive impression although of course if I were reporting from the other side, that might be different. I could report what was happening, but I couldn't be biased on one side or another. That was MBC's policy and I thought it was a good one.

I picked up a copy of the paper and was appalled. There I was, on the front page, quoted as giving an account of northern victories that Saleh himself would have found flattering, and dismissing the southern fighters as separatist terrorists. I hadn't said any of that. It wasn't simply a distortion of my views - it was a pack of lies.

I finally understood Tony Benn. I'd interviewed the Grand Old Man of British socialism a couple of years before, and he'd switched on a tape recorder when our interview began. 'Nothing personal,' he apologised 'I always keep a record interviews. I was a professional broadcaster myself once, and I know how easy it is to tweak the content so that it means exactly what you didn't want it to mean.'

I wished I'd done the same. In London, they told me to calm down. 'Don't worry, we know you wouldn't have said it. We've seen your reports.'

But in Yemen, the damage was done. Shortly before we left, Foreign Ministry invited all the media in Sana'a to lunch. One of the influential Yemenis present was an extremely wealthy fellow who owned great swathes of fertile land and supported Saleh's army with money. There was a discussion about the piece in the paper. He was a mean-spirited, vulgar fellow, I thought. His cronies were derisive when I told them what I'd really said to the journalist.

'You can't be in the middle,' one of them told me. 'If you don't support one side you support the other.'

'Exactly,' said the millionaire, staring coldly at me from small piggy eyes. 'Unbiased my arse. It's a blind. Green paper talks.'

'What?' Puzzled, I looked at Basindawa. 'Green paper?'

'Greenbacks. Dollars,' he said.

'You mean he thinks I'm being bribed?'

He pulled a face.

'Wait a minute please,' I said to the man.

Abed was sitting next to me. 'Can you get the float out of my jacket?' My photographer's jacket had pockets all round, and the one at the back had our float in it - the petty cash and expenses we needed for the trip. I leaned forward as Abed struggled to get the thick roll of cash out, and handed it to me.

I put it on the table. It was somewhere between $17,000 and $20,000. 'You mean this?' I asked. 'This is for the team: me, Abed and Nick. I am an MBC employee who gets a salary. They are self-employed contractors. I need to pay all our expenses on the assignment and that's what this is for. I pay for our hotel rooms and taxis with it, and we are all entitled to spend a certain amount every day for food and drink. And there's a big contingency element, because this is a war zone and anything could happen; we might even need a helicopter. I have to keep every single receipt and account for every cent of it when I get back to London. That is what employees do.'

'That's what you say.'

'What do you know about it? What are you insinuating? Put your money where your mouth is. If you employ me and provide expenses for my assignments I'll do the same. I'll do a report on television for you and MBC will put it out. Just as long as you don't expect me to take your side or the other side.'

The man snorted dismissively. I was extremely angry.

'You try to humiliate me. You don't know what you're talking about. Just shut up. Don't talk rubbish... Or I will bring my Algerians out to see you and you won't like it.' Everybody laughed but I hadn't finished yet. 'Listen, I report what I see on the ground and so does a different MBC guy in the south. The war is your problem. We're here for a few weeks and we leave. Don't accuse MBC of bias.'

I'd done my best to make him see how I worked, but it was hopeless. I was struggling to challenge a mind-set that had evolved through decades of growing rich. He'd lived a life in which self-interest always won and bribery, one way or another, was necessary to get things done.

Chapter 5

Unintended consequences

The Yemeni War was my calling card. I was from then onwards a war correspondent. Thanks to Nick, I'd been able to learn on the job. And I went on learning, fortunately never making any life-threatening mistakes.

I learned a lot in London as well. I watched how the media works and I went to broadcasting conferences. Western culture is different from ours. People in Britain know that they don't have to accept a given version of the truth. They can choose. Everyone, from beggar to king, is allowed to judge and question. TV and radio and the press reflect this questioning, and reinforce it as well. It's ingrained. Mothers don't respond to their little child's 'Why?' with 'Because I say so!' or patronise them with parables. They do their best to say what they really think.

This had first struck me in Leicester, as a student. A woman I knew had a daughter of four. One day we all walked to the park. The little girl said

'Hacene can I ask you a question?'

'Yes.'

'Do you like my mum, or do you love her?'

I was taken aback. A little girl in the Arab world is not supposed to think about such things, far less ask about them. What was going on here? I pulled myself together and asked

'What's the difference?'

'If you like her,' she said seriously 'you just kiss her. If you love her, you marry her.'

I was flabbergasted. But then I thought 'education, education, education'. That's how it works. You think, you ask questions, you get answers and you test them.

We tried to do no-holds-barred, western style television at all times and mostly we succeeded. I admit we were aware of certain 'sensitivities'. We didn't, for instance, mention the Saudis exiled in London who wanted the Saudi royal family deposed and replaced by a democratic republic. There was a tacit red line that we couldn't cross. We pushed it as far as we could go, but we knew when it would snap.

BBC journalists, true to their tradition, avoided self-censorship. They didn't believe in it. They were open to all shades of opinion because otherwise, they knew, they could never be fully trusted as a source of news.

Not long after I was in Yemen, two Saudi princes were inspired to start their own satellite channel in Arabic, in collaboration with the BBC. Their company was named Orbit Communications Corporation. It was a subsidiary of a huge Saudi parent company, and it was based in Rome. Programmes on BBC Arabic-language TV would be produced in London by a team of about 150 BBC staff, but Orbit would pay their salaries.

BBC Worldwide was only too pleased to have its own Arabic channel to publicise the BBC brand for nothing, all over the Middle East and North Africa. The Orbit contract would be for ten years and in that time not a penny would come from British public money. In order not to pollute their brand the BBC insisted, of course, on editorial control. That condition was iron-bound into the contract. Editorial decisions by staff could not be challenged or changed by the owners.

The Saudi princes didn't take any notice of that clause. It was a legal formality, they assumed, and since BBC was owned by the British government it was bomb-proof. Why would a state-run TV station even think of doing anything controversial?

Transmissions began, from the old BBC TV Centre at White City. Within quite a short time a new face began to appear in the studio, explaining current events in Saudi Arabia as he saw them. This happened to be Mohammed Al-Massari, the leader of the Saudi republicans in London. The Saudis were furious. What did these people think they were doing, giving air-time to that man? They expressed their anger. The BBC must respect cultural sensitivities! This was unacceptable.

Predictably, the BBC refused to be bullied. There was skirmish after skirmish. The politics and outlook of the Saudis were contentious so they broadcast all points of view, including those that were hostile. This caused discomfort. The Saudi royal family could not accustom themselves to such lack of respect. It seems that the final straw broke the camel's back when an episode of the BBC's popular weekly documentary *Panorama*, highly critical of Saudi Arabia, was rebroadcast on BBC Arabic TV.

'Who owns this channel?' King Fahd asked.

He was told. He rang the princes and told them to knock heads together. They tried to get the BBC to adapt to Saudi views. John Tusa was in charge of the Arabic service at the time and refused, because the integrity and brand of the BBC could not be compromised.

The King asked How much will it cost to cancel the contract? They told him. (Gossip named a figure over £100 million; I don't know.) And on 21st April 1996, two years since the deal was done, the plug was pulled at one hour's notice.

The TV journalists, suddenly unemployed, mounted a demonstration. They wanted compensation. The NUJ got involved. The law was on their side. A deal was done; they were paid off.

There is a red line.

Then came the unintended consequence: Al Jazeera.

The al-Thanis in Qatar were not as nervous as the Sauds. They came along and offered work in Doha, and in London, to the rebellious ex-employees. This looked like a one-nil victory to Qatar. What had been a war of words, then a stand-off over a border dispute, had turned into a media war between Sauds and Al Thanis. MBC had never felt a need to compete with the Qataris or sideline them, but rivalry now became an issue. In 1996, Al Jazeera started to broadcast from Doha: funded by Qatar, staffed by ex-BBC Arabic journalists.

The implications for MBC would be considerable, but I didn't see that coming.

Chapter 6

Futility

Every morning, at a news channel, there's an editorial meeting in the newsroom. The news editor will have decided what the main stories for the day will be. Those will be assigned. The foreign editor will then make suggestions. Our foreign editor, Amanda, spoke eight languages and would have been at work since since the crack of dawn talking to our staff in other time zones. By the time we sat down for the daily meeting she'd already have telephoned most of the correspondents worldwide. 'What have you got for us today?' she'd say, and the MBC person in Paris, or Jerusalem, or wherever would tell her what was going on and needed covering. She'd listen to all of them and come up with her own shortlist. After the editorial meeting, she'd be able to call back and say 'run with it' or 'don't'. If your story was turned down you'd probably go out and shoot some local item of interest that could be used at any time, while keeping on the alert for another story for tomorrow.

London-based correspondents like me had a responsibility to suggest stories if there was something of note that needed covering. The editor could say yes or turn it down. I had to pitch something of significance to viewers; it had to be visually interesting; and I needed to suggest other items that I could cover in the course of the assignment - after all, the channel would be paying for my time, and that of the team, so we had to be productive. We undertook to work every hour we could for a pre-arranged, budgetable duration, which would keep the administrators happy and make it more likely that we'd get jobs in future; producers cannot work with people who habitually go over budget. Often we would shoot enough to tell one story three times from different angles, so that the 3pm, 6pm and 9pm news slots would all be different.

I always put my ideas in writing to the editor, not just as a record but because that helps to clarify one's thoughts. If the criteria were met, but the answer was still no, then if I genuinely felt the editor was missing a trick here, I would try to think my case through and make it again, but better.

That's how I ended up in Chechnya.

I hadn't taken much notice of the news about Chechnya, although it had been making headlines, on and off, for a year. What our news editor understood, and that time I didn't, was that historically, there'd been an uneasy relationship between the Chechens and the Russian state apparatus, and now that the USSR had collapsed, and the Russian Federation had replaced it, the Chechens wanted – not necessarily independence, but more autonomy. The Russians were alarmed. As far as they were concerned these were dangerous separatists. One prominent Chechen was even talking up a Chechen-Dagestan Union which would have cut Russia off from the Caspian coast and threatened the security of Russia's gas pipeline from states further east.

Nor did Russia want a potential Islamic state in quite such a strategically important place; most Chechens and Dagestanis were Muslims. Our main audience thought of themselves as belonging to the Gulf, the eastern Mediterranean and North Africa, while in fact there is a large diaspora on every continent (I haven't tested that generalisation in Antarctica or the North Pole, but I'm more or less right). So this David and Goliath story about Chechnya and Russia was of interest to us.

In the late summer of '96, militant Chechens drove the Russians out of their capital, Grozny. Later on, when Putin came to power, there would be a second Chechen war; but we didn't know that. Right now there was a lull in hostilities, a window of opportunity in which we might be able to film there. So this was a story for MBC to run. Anne - our awesome fixer, who was one of those people with a massive contacts book gained over decades of work in TV and film, and a job title like Executive Production Manager – duly called our Moscow correspondent and asked him to go down to Chechnya and report. He said it would be impossible. The Russians weren't permitting journalists. He went on saying this. And it would be useless to send somebody from London, he said, because the Foreign Ministry wouldn't issue accreditation.

Anne liked a challenge. We'd all seen footage from Chechnya: not much, but people were getting in. 'You go ahead and come up with the idea,' she said. 'I'll see what I can do.'

If you want to get an ambitious idea past a News Editor you don't offer to take crew and equipment four thousand miles to do one piece to camera from alongside a rocket launcher. You suggest a few different angles, in hope that he'll trust you enough to know that when you get there, even if nothing is quite what you expected, you'll be able to find enough original takes on a subject to make it worth the expense. I made up my mind to try.

I had to start with research. I didn't even know that most of the native locals were Sunni Muslims, and had been for hundreds of years. In fact I had to look on a map to find the place. It's in the North Caucasus, between the Black Sea and the Caspian: a strategically important location, one of the major land links between the Russian Federation and the Middle East. The people of Chechnya and its neighbours, Ingushetia and Dagestan, are unusual in having strong genetic links to Iron Age people of the Fertile Crescent, that scimitar-shaped cradle of western civilisation that flourished between Egypt, Syria and the Gulf ten thousand years ago.

I needed a bit more background than this, because all the news reports I'd seen were snapshots rather than in-depth analysis. I was impressed by an English academic I saw on the BBC and Channel 4 who seemed to know exactly what he was talking about, so I invited him to the MBC studios in Battersea to talk me through it. He gave me an excellent summary of the situation and the history. I also managed to establish contact with an Arabic-speaking Chechen professor at Riyadh University. I gave my questions to our correspondent there and he got an interview with the professor and sent me the tape.

The Chechens had their reasons to loathe Russia. For one thing, they'd squabbled with their powerful neighbour on and off for about five hundred years before finally being annexed to it in the 1870s. (One of the stranger things I discovered was that the guards at the royal palace in Jordan are traditionally Chechen, their ancestors having fled to the Ottoman Empire when the Russians occupied their homeland.) In the Second World War Stalin deported tens of thousands of Chechens to Siberia because he suspected them of collaborating with the Germans.

In the 1950s Khruschev allowed the survivors to return home, but indignation and resentment remained; their state was run by Russians and their children were offered an inferior education. Chechens resented Russian incomers taking all the good jobs.

After the USSR's disintegration, Russia was weakened. In September of '91 Chechnya declared independence and set up its own government under Dzhokhar Dudayev, a Chechen former commander in the Russian Air Force. After this the discrimination was in the opposite direction, and Russians started to leave. This loss of a skilled workforce affected Chechnya's economy. Civil war broke out between Dudayev's supporters and a Moscow-backed opposition. Nobody challenged the idea of an independent Chechnya – independence wasn't the problem. It was all about who ran the country: a leader who had popular support, or a Moscow-backed puppet.

Russia sent troops to the border and skirmishes began. By 1995 these had intensified into a brutal war, with Grozny, the capital, besieged and under devastating bombardment from the air. The Russians had the fire power, the technology, the numbers; the ethnic Chechens were essentially guerrillas, but they were winning.

There were misgivings inside Russia about this kind of war. Russian troops had already been driven out of Afghanistan with devastating loss of life because it was hard to defeat well-armed fighters who could hide in their own terrain. Ordinary Russians did not want to sacrifice another generation in a long-drawn-out, futile war.

So once I'd listened to the professor and read around the subject, I went back to Anne.

'Any luck?'

'Of course. Would I let you down? I've got you some Chechens. They'll meet you off the plane and sort you out.' What a woman. I'd already dreamed up a project that would result in at least ten meaty reports so I put them to the News Editor and he agreed. We'd be a three-man crew: Raef, Lee and me.

There were no direct flights from Heathrow to Grozny at the time. In fact there were no direct flights from anywhere to Grozny, so the crew and I would have to get accreditation through the Russian Embassy in London and travel via Moscow.

While our paperwork was crawling through the system we set off for Oslo. We went there first, because I wanted to cover a conference where the Chechnya conflict would be discussed. The Norwegians provided general views of the proceedings and it was up to us to doorstep whoever we could. A press conference was held at the end, and plenty of European politicians were there, including Heads of State and a number of Russian journalists.

The Russian media were paying special attention to Vladimir Putin. He was already being talked about as a potential successor to Boris Yeltsin. He swaggered out, looking, as usual, as if he knew more than anybody else but you'd have to kill him before he'd tell you. He had minders with him, holding their hands up in warning - 'No Filming. No Filming.' I stepped diffidently into his path and said, in English,

'Mr Putin I don't ask for an interview. I'm an Arab journalist from MBC London. I need permission to come to Russia and make a report about Chechnya and I wonder if you can help me.'

'If I can,' he said affably. 'There should be no problem.'

He beckoned to an aide, who approached as the Great Pretender moved on, and took my card.

Back in London I took the tube to the Embassy in Kensington and they gave me a Moscow number to call. I went back to the office and rang the Foreign Press Bureau of the Russian Foreign Ministry. A gravelly voice said

'Yes, your application is with us. You want a guide and interpreter also? He is $100 a day, he is very good, many people use him.'

'Will he come with us to Grozny?'

'No problem.'

'I will check with my office. I think that will be OK.'

'Send me all the travel documents and passport copies by fax and call me in two hours.'

Anne had been doing this sort of thing forever. She kept photocopies of all crew documents, so she faxed the whole bundle and I called him back.

'It's fixed,' he said. 'You can pick everything up from the Embassy in London. And when you arrive in Moscow, call me and bring me a bottle of good wine.' We took him three bottles of decent wine and $100 in cash. I could have picked his brains about ways to get to Chechnya but by that time it was unnecessary. The wheels were oiled.

Even the long-established TV channels have to trust the correspondent to find the best way into a war zone. The media facilitate everything, but because you are the one who is travelling, and who is likely to have contacts, the final decisions are yours. You're competing with the rest of the media pack to find and use good contacts. In this case, I didn't have a single Chechen in my address book. I had no idea how to get into Grozny. But Anne's Chechen company would make all the arrangements to get us there.

'We will look after them,' they'd told her in thick accents 'and we will bring them out.'

It cost a certain amount of money, of course, but you have to trust people. When we came out of the Customs and Immigration hall we saw a tall dark fellow in a belted black leather coat holding up a card with MBC on it. He led us to two gleaming black sedans. We met five other guys who looked like his brothers. They seized the equipment and started loading it into the cars. Lee, the English cameraman, didn't look happy but I didn't speak the language and neither did Raef. These guys had hardly a word of English between them and we hadn't arranged to meet the interpreter until tomorrow morning. The driver turned to us and made money signals, rubbing finger and thumb together. 'You pay us.'

That wasn't the deal at all.

'Ah - Anne - in MBC London, Anne pays after.' I made this as clear as possible in sign language. 'You help, Anne pays.'

He looked puzzled. The others were gathering round.

I said, with a lot of pointing and gesturing, 'What do you do for us?' He understood that. 'We take you – ' he indicated everywhere between here and the Black Sea with a wide sweep of his leather-clad arm –'to Grozny. We help your work.'

'Good, good.'

'We help you see many people. You pay now, dollars.'

'No, no dollars for that. You talked with Anne.' He said something in Russian to the others, who looked fed up.

I was not at ease but they'd got our tens of thousands of pounds worth of kit, so we got into the first car with two of them while the four others followed in the second.

Our hotel was magnificent, an old one of the sparkling-chandelier, wide-red-carpeted-staircase variety. The Chechens made it clear that they would be back tomorrow, which was fine since we'd have an interpreter then. We had three rooms on the top floor and we all went to bed quite early.

At one in the morning I was awoken by persistent rapping on the door and a low voice saying something. I fought through a fog of sleep to make sense of it. 'To reception please. All guests come to reception now.' I heard knocking on the door next door to mine, and talking, and so on from further away.

I couldn't smell smoke, so this made no sense, but as I could hear other people being woken up and leaving their rooms I shrugged an overcoat over my pyjamas, picked up small valuables, and was out of the room in twenty seconds. Guests were hurrying down the corridor and stairs and we all gathered in the foyer, yawning.

There we waited. There was no information at all from the staff. Nobody seemed to know what was going on. Moscow was not the safest place at the time, since Chechens had pursued their fight to the capital and there had been a bomb on the underground. But there was no sign of trouble here.

At 3am we were allowed to go back. I woke up tired at the usual time in the morning and went down to breakfast. Lee was at a table reading the English-language paper. 'Here's what that was all about,' he said, and showed me the front page. BOMB IN METROPOL HOTEL. There was a library shot of the hotel and a photograph of a room where there'd been an explosion. Unconfirmed reports indicated that a Chechen mafia suspect had been supposed to be staying there. In our rooms on the top floor we hadn't heard a thing - not even a fire engine.

When the interpreter arrived, so did all six of the Chechens. I'm not sure how they felt about him, since they must have guessed he was from the Foreign Press Bureau, but if they mistrusted him they didn't say so. I told them we'd call them when we needed them. We would be staying in Moscow for a few days since we had to get our accreditation, and film some stories from Moscow. After that, we'd meet them again. They left looking disgruntled.

Our friendly wine-drinker in the Press Bureau didn't suggest subjects for us to film; I had half-expected that he might be nosy or try to tell us what to do, but there was none of that. We were watched by security people when we went out to record vox pops but that was all. There were street demonstrations in Red Square at the time. The withdrawal from Grozny had been a defeat. The old Communists were disgusted and noisily protested. However the war wasn't over, and other demonstrators were anxious because Russia seemed likely to lose still more soldiers. They wanted negotiation rather than a further show of strength.

Our interpreter was with us all the time.

'Will there be any objection to our filming the demonstrators?'

'No,' he said. 'None at all.'

I had the baby-boomer's suspicion of the Russian security apparatus; for the first quarter of a century of my life Russia had been the biggest totalitarian state in the world after China. However, we made our first report about the demonstration and nobody stopped us. Key political opponents of Boris Yeltsin were only too happy to exploit the protests and when I saw one of them talking to the crowd I interviewed him. I got our interpreter to make a written translation from the tape afterwards, and had it checked by a Russian-speaking Syrian from the Kuwaiti Embassy. It was accurate.

I didn't wonder that people were discontented. The economy was polarised. Stupendous fortunes were being made by a tiny élite, but in every market you saw gnarled old women selling their own possessions for a few kopeks.

We sent the first report back via Reuters and it looked fabulously exotic, with snow on the onion domes of St Basil's Cathedral and Slavic faces framed in fur. Having established ourselves in Moscow, we talked to our Chechens with the interpreter's help. We would fly to the Caucasus and land in Ingushetia, its partner state, where there was a media centre.

Chechnya itself was still a war zone but a driver would take us in. When we started working in Grozny, we were to contact these Moscow Chechens and they would arrange for us to talk to the right people.

Our three-man crew, and the interpreter who made four, boarded an old Russian rustbucket and flew south-east for six hours. We landed amid snowy, well-tended, pleasantly rolling countryside. The press were housed in something like a summer camp: chalets around the main hall of a sports centre. The chalets were heated and had been made ready for us, although four people had to squeeze into each one.

Visnews, as we all still called it although it had been bought by Reuters, provided the satellite link. In neighbouring chalets were journalists from Denmark, Britain, America, France, Germany, Holland, Japan and probably a few other places. We would stay for a couple of weeks, and in that time I saw Brent Sadler from CNN, Christiane Amanpour and other well-known faces. Even MBC's own Moscow correspondent turned up for a few days – forced into it, I suppose, when we started sending material back. We didn't socialise with him. Numbers fluctuated, but every night about twenty of us ate together in a refectory where elderly ladies served us bread and home-made soup.

Every day we rose at the crack of dawn to cross the border into Chechnya to film. The four of us, and all our kit, travelled with a local driver in a cramped van. When MBC's Moscow crew came they were interested in the fighting, but from the start I was keener to cover the impact on ordinary people.

On the first day in a new place you're acutely aware of details. The border, when we reached it, was a wide river. We saw that the main bridge had been hit by some sort of missile and was now impassable. Whenever you have a crew you exploit every opportunity you can to record something, so this was a story and we stopped. I did a piece to camera with the beautiful snowy countryside and damaged bridge behind me, saying how the Russians had done this to cut off the supply of arms to Chechnya. We wrapped that up and carried on, gingerly driving over a makeshift pontoon bridge, and then stopped to interview people in the first village. 'There was no problem here before,' they claimed. 'We always went back and forth. We always have. There've never been any guns going over – the Russians were completely wrong about that.'

The van driver wouldn't take us to the centre of Grozny because there was intermittent fighting there, so we had to shoulder the equipment and walk the last few miles – and do the same five hours later so that he could pick us up.

When he stopped the van in the outskirts we could see dereliction all around. There was nobody about; everything was quiet. The remains of Grozny looked like second world photographs of Hiroshima or Dresden or the London Docks: a greyish moonscape of tumbled concrete and wood and debris, with a few buildings standing isolated, balconies smashed but roofs still on. You hoped there would be nobody inside when they were used for target practice.

We trudged along dodging rocks and holes and trying not to lose the road altogether. We had set off from the press centre at six and it was now after seven in the morning; we wouldn't be here for more than a couple of weeks and we had to use very available minute to produce something for broadcasting. We could hear shelling in the distance, but apart from that there was quiet. There were almost no vehicles. After a few miles we thought we might have arrived at what had once been the centre. There were more people about, more stray dogs, and a bad smell when we occasionally passed human remains. The ruins were more substantial here, looking as if they'd once been brutalist administration blocks of the kind you saw in Moscow. Less than half a mile away we could see one monstrous building, almost untouched. The interpreter said it was the Presidential Palace.

Before we walked any further I switched on Radio Moscow, which broadcast in English, to find out whether there had been any major change we didn't know about. The Presidential Palace in Grozny had been occupied by Russian soldiers, said the announcer.

We couldn't see any unusual activity around it so we got closer. When we were within 300 metres, we saw that the Chechen flag was flying over the building and there were no Russians at all. We set up so that Raef could pull out from his focus on the flag, hanging on its flagpole against a bright blue sky, to show me standing there doing the piece to camera. I was able to say that Radio Moscow was wrong, and the Chechens still held the palace. It was a nice piece and I was almost through when two bullets flew past inches from my head. I dived. (I edited that part out. I thought my mother, at home in Algeria, might have a heart attack if she saw it.)

On rubble-strewn streets we saw isolated pedestrians picking their way over snow and debris, half-empty buses occasionally, and our first Chechen patrol. We'd later discover that these were everywhere, policing the city. They were groups of seven formidably tall and sturdy Chechen rebels walking in formation, one in front and the others in two lines of three behind, wearing white plastic boiler suits as camouflage in the snow. They had no helmets, just headbands with *There is one God and Mohamed is his Prophet* on them in Arabic. Each man carried about fifty kilos of weaponry, including RPGs and AK-47s.

They always nodded and said 'Salaam Aleichem' as they passed. I asked why they were organised in groups of seven and they replied drily 'It works.' I suspect that many had been conscripted as young men into the Russian army. There were foreigners among them. We heard the name of a Chechen leader called Khattab, who was from Jordan, and one we met turned out to be an anti-Russian Ukrainian - not even a Muslim. They called themselves mujahidin.

Chechens are Sunni, and wealthy and resourceful. Theirs is a small rich country and they knew how to hide. The Russians had relied mainly on air power, so they had had no difficulty in flattening Grozny, but they could never match Chechen guerrillas on the ground. Yeltsin knew this, which is why he was prepared to enter peace talks.

Back at the press centre, we rang the number the Chechen Six had given us. 'We'll make sure you're safe,' they had said. 'We will arrange interviews.'

They were true to their word. In the days that followed we interviewed mujahidin leaders and were taken to see some Russian prisoners of war. We saw about fifty young soldiers being held in the basement of a ruined building. I gave cigarettes to some of them. Then I interviewed a Chechen leader with a line of uniformed captives in the background. I asked him about their treatment. He was talking to me in Russian. 'We are fair,' translated the interpreter. In the background, one of the Russian soldiers stepped forward. Over the interviewee the interpreter was saying 'We respect the Geneva convention at all times.' Behind him a Chechen seized the soldier, delivered a hard left hook to the jaw and shoved him out of shot. I was laughing and the interviewee turned to see what I was looking at. He said something else. 'There are always exceptional circumstances,' said the interpreter smoothly.

The whole episode cut together beautifully.

The prisoners were at least safe underground. Outside, we were always at risk because the shelling hadn't stopped. There was almost no traffic, and we were walking with all our gear around Grozny without protection. Everywhere was evidence of brutality, trauma and humanitarian disaster. In one street we walked between two bodies, one on the left, one on the right; a couple of old, frail people, a man and a woman. We were very affected and started filming. A passer by told us

'They were Russians - trying to get away.'

'Did the Russian air strikes kill them?'

'I wouldn't know. They're victims, whoever did it.'

We saw dogs eating the unburied bodies and elderly people hobbling along on sticks, looking for food and water, under fire from shells. They would go to a snowy fountain where the sprays of water had turned to crystalline ice, and try to snap some off to take away. It was a beautiful picture, but immensely sad.

I tried not to get emotionally involved but we saw terrible things. There were gangs of feral children, orphaned and brutalised but somehow surviving as scavengers, like the dogs. Once there was a disembodied head, hanging from a window.

Most of the media stopped going because it was so dangerous. Russian planes flew low over the city, which was one reason there were few vehicles; cars made an easy target.

Our footage was powerful. It was the first time Russians and Arabs in conflict had seen one another. The Reuters editors began rushing over when we got back in the afternoons. 'What did you get?' They wanted to use it, and MBC in London said as long as we retained the right to broadcast it first, they'd do a deal.

Thanks to the Chechen Six, we were able to go out in the country and talk to some of the locals there. I was surprised and delighted to find that everything was familiar. The farmers kept cows and donkeys and dogs and lived in low villas facing inwards to a busy courtyard, just like the ones I'd known as a child in Algeria. In the remoter areas these households could have passed for Berber, with the women in colourful shawls patterned with vivid flowers, embroidered bodices and long skirts. Everyone sat on a cloth on the ground to eat food that was grilled or stewed over a wood fire. I was astonished to bite into a local version of merguez, the spicy lamb sausage from North Africa.

On another day, looking for something to eat, we found a countrywoman on her own beside the road, selling food to travellers from a handcart. She was boiling sheep's chitlings, chicken parts and a sheep's head in buckets. Lee looked horrified when we identified what everything was. He quickly chose the chicken. The sheep's head had been boiled for hours and the broth smelled delicious, so we three went for that. Lee wrinkled his face in disgust.

'I need a drink to get me through this.'

'Vodka,' said the interpreter.

'Has she got Smirnoff?'

The old lady had a stock of bottles. They all contained clear liquid of indefinable origin and dubious labelling. We made a show of scrutinising them seriously. 'No.'

'We'll buy you a bottle of that one,' I said, pointing at random.

Lee poured himself half a tumbler full, then hesitated. 'Will it make me go blind?'

'Shouldn't think so.'

He sipped it, coughed and his eyes watered. 'Not bad at all.' He tried again, alternating attempts at his 'vodka' with cautious bites at a chicken gizzard.

Raef, fishing in his bowl, retrieved a piece of meat with an eye in. 'Hey! I got lucky.'

'Oh NO - take it away.' Lee was turning green.

'No!' protested Raef. 'Look, it's lovely - There's nothing to worry about - See, this is how you take the eye out.'

Lee groaned and grimaced.

'That's the best part,' confirmed the interpreter. 'Look, they're delicious.' He popped the other eye in his mouth. I thought Lee would faint.

Commerce had survived. Colourfully dressed Chechen women were selling sweets along the road outside Grozny. They had the matter-of-fact resilience of people who took hardship for granted: drawing water, collecting firewood, feeding the animals, cooking and sewing for sixteen hours a day, all year round; that was their whole life. Their families had never been accepted for the best schools, or invited to the best houses, or given important jobs, because Russians got those advantages.

The men, farmers and guerrillas alike, wore big long sheepskin jerkins and Chechen karakul hats of tightly curled baby lamb, which were like an astrakhan hat but taller, and slightly wider at the top like a flowerpot, without the typically Russian ear-flaps and peak.

They were wild fellows. We filmed some Chechen and Dagestani men who were doing a traditional dance in what was left of central Grozny, near the Palace. In their high hats, sheepskins and boots, they began to dance to musicians making music with flute and tambour. Their movement grew faster and fiercer, and as they whirled and stamped they became more and more excited until they were in a kind of religious frenzy. I had seen footage of Dzhokhar Dudayev himself dancing like that at the independence announcement.

Most ordinary Chechens fled Grozny because of the Russian bombardment and escaped to stay with family in the country. As strangers, we could only dive into the nearest available cellar. We'd switch a Maglite on never knowing whether we'd find rats, cadavers or refugees from bombardment like ourselves. Usually we found elderly Russians who had spent their whole lives in Chechnya. Once, we found a group of ancient men and women, bundled up, holding their wrinkled old hands to a tiny fire of wood and cardboard. Our torch picked out a small wallet on the ground. It had exactly one rouble in it.

They could not escape. They had no money, and were not strong enough to walk across any borders. I made a report about them; they didn't mind. I used to carry chocolate, for energy, and I gave it to one of the old ladies. It was all I had. She said something and clasped my arm with tears in her eyes. Our interpreter spoke.

'She says you came all the way from London and you give us sweets. Your life will be lit by a candle until you die.'

We were making our living from their tragedy. As usual I felt a sense of unfairness, of unequal exchange. But we could do good. We may even have influenced public opinion. After I met that group I said, in my piece to camera -

'The Russians are not killing Chechens in Grozny. Yeltsin is bombing his own people, and it's pointless. There are other ways to deal with this conflict.'

Every morning we went out, looking for stories; every afternoon we left the city, found our driver along the road and were taken back to edit the footage in the media centre and transmit it to London. One day we went to the second city, Gudermes. We saw a woman walking through the street wheeling a steaming, lidded metal vat on a little cart in the street. The interpreter went to have a word with her. He explained what she was doing, so we followed and saw it. She pushed open the door of a big old institution and pulled the little cart inside. The building smelled sour, and looked dirty, and although there was glass in the windows it was bitterly cold.

I could hear low cries and moans and she led us to people huddled in one big dormitory.

This was not a hospital but an asylum. There were twenty or thirty inmates: old, shivering, toothless and utterly naked, with only filthy blankets to cover them. They were Chechen, Russian, Ukrainian - who could tell? She couldn't, and it didn't matter. She ladled soup from the vat into bowls. Every person had some, and those who could not spoon it into their mouths, she helped.

The staff had simply run away. Every morning she made cabbage soup and took it to the asylum to keep the starving patients alive.

We went back the following day, to film her making the soup and taking it through the streets, so that it made a story, with a beginning and a middle. As for the end, who knew? This was the impact of the war. It was impossible not to be angry. I felt that no cause could justify treating people like this.

We did do some good. MBC's coverage alerted Islamic Relief to the needs of people in Chechnya, and when they came they tried to distribute food to all who needed it.

We were a long way from Moscow, yet every afternoon, when MBC put me on air, I needed to be aware of what was going on elsewhere. A correspondent has to keep up with world events and listen to what other teams are talking about, and if you're the only journalist with a tiny crew you need extra diligence and initiative to do that. CNN and the BBC had brought more people than we had and could call on more resources. Their correspondents had researchers and other people back at base, whose job it was to brief the guys who happened to be out in the field. I had only my own eyes and ears to rely on most of the time. Sometimes I would stop and listen to somebody from another channel doing a live broadcast in French or English; that helped.

Not long after I left, the first Chechen war was still at an impasse when Djhokhar Dudayev was killed.

The Russians had not been able to find him, but they did it in the end by tricking a third party.

The Moroccan government had volunteered their Ambassador's services as a mediator. The Russians therefore invited this gentleman to the Kremlin, promising to provide a competent interpreter to convey the phone conversation between himself and Dudayev. His aim was to persuade the Chechen leader to enter into negotiations, through him, with the Russians. The telephone link was made and he talked to Dudayev in good faith.

Dudayev had been led to believe that both the Arabic-speaking interpreter and the Moroccan Ambassador were speaking from the Moroccan Embassy. The conversation was complex and of course, took twice as long as usual because of the work the interpreter had to do. So the Russian military had plenty of time to identify Dudayev's position and launch an RPG at it. Within an hour of the conversation's end, he was killed by a rocket strike.

Leaderless, the Chechens lost focus. They renewed their efforts to achieve independence with a second war later, but at time of writing their state remains a Russian satellite.

Chapter 7

Making History

In my first few years at MBC, when I saw conflict in other parts of the world I always, consciously or unconsciously, compared their situations with those I knew from the two countries that had influenced me most: Algeria and England. In 1994 both had begun peace processes.

Algeria had been good to me. When I was growing up in the 1960s and 1970s, it was a newly independent country with a government dedicated to providing opportunity for all. The priority was to eradicate illiteracy, because by driving the French out, Algerians had done what the Chechens would do later - they had driven out the educated class they most needed. The French, in well over a hundred years of occupation, had provided clean water, the rule of law, French language and culture, and elements of a constitution that the independent Algeria would later adopt; but these advantages were not available to the mass of Algerians. They were enjoyed almost exclusively by the *pieds noirs*, urban bourgeoisie of French origin. The French had done very little to educate the many Algerian children who were brought up in in the countryside. However this was rectified by a left-leaning government when I was a child.

The day after Independence in 1963, the Algerian government had instituted Sonatrach: the national oil company. It was like switching on an engine and knowing that the supply of petrol was guaranteed. Oil represented the national money supply. The Ministry of Education in Algiers delegated control of local education and utilities to each of 48

Departments, and gave them their own budget which was topped up by local taxes. We had to attend classes from the age of six, and were generously served. We paid a negligible amount - about a penny to have breakfast at school and tuppence for lunch. If you worked hard and passed your exams for admission to university, your course fees were paid by the government and you could apply for a grant for accommodation.

This sounds almost utopian but there was political conflict. Our socialist rulers were actively hostile to enterprise, believing that it increased inequality. Farmers were therefore organised in co-operatives, which demotivated them. The years between '79 and '89 were called the Black Decade because people were poor and discontented. There had been a levelling down, rather than a levelling up.

Because Algeria was reliant on oil, when the oil price plummeted everybody suffered. The ruling party were defensive and as is usual in North Africa and the Middle East, the army attacked civilians who made any kind of public protest. That was the kind of response that I'd seen on my visit to Algiers as a student and nothing much had changed when I began work in TV. Intellectuals were especially suspect, and a lot of journalists emigrated rather than risk imprisonment.

Free education and low-cost health care were excellent, but that was where the benevolence ended. Sonatrach was safely out in the desert. Our rulers used most of its revenues to pay the army but consistently failed to help the impoverished civilian population. Only an élite, close to the centre of power, seemed to be living suspiciously well. Everything indicated corruption at all levels of government.

Then came the moment when somebody in the Italian Parliament, of all places, mentioned the Energy Minister's name in association with the disappearance of $26 billion. The Prime Minister of Algeria happened to come to London, and I wanted to know if it was true that such a sum had, indeed, vanished. I sat him down with the camera running, and asked the question.

'Twenty-six billion?' he said. 'More like fifty-two billion. It's all contracts.'

What he meant was, the Energy Ministry would award a contract for, say, $1 billion and the Minister who assigned it would add a 10% *pourboire* for himself. It mounts up. As a famous American once said, 'A billion here, a billion there, and pretty soon you're talking serious money.'

The Prime Minister knew this from Military Intelligence. The heads of the foreign oil and construction companies were called in but nothing happened, and by that time the Energy Minister himself had vanished, overseas.

Algeria was a democracy of sorts, and the Government could be voted out. Historically, there was no particular fondness for Islamist political parties but in the late 1980s they benefited from protest votes and won local elections. This gave them a chance to show what they could do at grass-roots level, and they used it.

The main social issue at the time was housing. In the cities, it was common to find two or even three generations of a family squeezed into a couple of rooms yet there were hundreds of empty apartments with piped water and electricity laid on. These were held by local politicians who bought support by giving them only to cronies.

Suddenly, in local elections all over Algeria, the Islamists won power. They looked at the waiting lists, identified empty apartments, opened them up and distributed them to the thousands who had suffered in cramped accommodation for years. After ten years of decreasing hope in growing cynicism, people would open a letter that said 'come and collect the keys.'

In 1989 there was a natural disaster: an earthquake near the coast in which thirty people died and hundreds were left homeless. The regime didn't call out the army to help. It was left to the Islamists to react fast with a big relief effort. They sent out vans full of food, issued people with tents for shelter, and earned a lot of respect.

If they could work wonders like this at local level they could surely transform the nation; so when the general election came, people voted Islamist. The Islamists won a majority in the first round.

This was a threat to the army, who had done well out of the ruling party and had a lot to lose. If the Islamists won the second round, the Army would no longer be in a position to manipulate their democratically elected bosses. Algeria has a Presidential system, like France and America, in which the Head of State holds a lot of power. President Chedli had three years of his Presidency left. He knew that the Islamists would probably dominate the Assembly, but was committed to democracy and decided to accept the result, whatever it was.

The generals were furious and told him to resign. Chedli refused, saying he would be perfectly prepared to work with the Islamists. The constitution required Algeria to have political parties and democratic elections, and sometimes this kind of thing would happen. The President had more control than the legislature in any case.

The army told him that they would not allow this. People said that the Generals were being manipulated by French and American interests alarmed at the prospect of an Islamic party in control of $20 billion in annual oil revenues; I don't know if that's true or not. But while this was being discussed, the second round of elections took place. International observers said it was well run. It resulted, as predicted, in a victory for the Islamist party.

The Army announced that the election was invalid, had all been a fix, and the result was cancelled. The President appeared on the 8pm news and told the nation that too much blood had been spilled in Algeria since the Revolution of 1954 and it was time now to find peace: he, personally, was not willing to preside over an unnecessary conflict; and with regret, he resigned.

The Generals took over. Once a country is under military rule, there really isn't much opportunity for dialogue, even with moderates. Over the next few years the Generals became known as the Eradicators. They simply eradicated opponents rather than enter into a discussion. Journalists were killed for telling the truth and very often nobody knew who had committed the murder; whether it was the army, or terrorist action by opponents of the army who by now were squabbling between themselves. It seemed you couldn't win, whatever position you took, so once again there was an exodus of middle class professionals, doctors and lawyers as well as media people. In the early 1990s over a million people left, usually for France or Canada. Yet again Algeria had alienated its most valuable human resource.

And of course Algerian State television could show none of this.

When I started with MBC, the Blood Decade was beginning - the civil war; and by that time I was able to see Algeria dispassionately. I genuinely wanted to know how this violence could have been prevented and how both sides could negotiate a compromise.

I compared the Algerian Government's response to the one I'd seen in Britain - which had been similar before, but had now moved on.

The British, at this time, were in conflict with the Catholic population in Northern Ireland. I'd been there often. Their army had begun with a heavy-handed response but the British politicians and Irish terrorists (or freedom fighters, if you like) were now talking each other.

It wasn't the same situation as the one in Algeria; the British army in northern Ireland were subservient to politicians. Few people in the rest of the British Isles really understood why people in Northern Ireland seemed to be squabbling over things that had happened centuries ago. Here's a simplified version of the 800-year background.

Most of the United Kingdom (England, Wales and Scotland) is one big island. Ireland is another island, about a third of its size, to the west of it. At a time, nearly a thousand years ago, when the Chinese and the Arabs were the most civilised and scientifically curious people on earth, and the people of northern Europe were little better than savages, English rulers took over the whole of Ireland. They went on to govern it for about eight hundred years, until 1922. They didn't treat the native Irish well, and for that and many other reasons, the Irish remained poor. However they stayed proudly united thanks to the Catholic Church, which gave them a flag to rally under, much as Islam is a banner for disaffected Arabs of today.

When (nearly five hundred years ago) the English left the Roman Catholic Church, the Irish did not; they maintained their loyalty in secret. As the years passed, in Ireland, English Protestants ruled Irish Catholics.

In 1689 the English imported a new Protestant King from Holland. He settled himself in London before sailed across to northern Ireland to put down a big rebellion there. And to make absolutely sure that he'd get no more trouble, he redistributed land in the conquered territory to thousands of Protestants, mostly from Scotland.

Discontent rumbled under the surface for generations. In 1922 the Irish, at the end of a terrorist campaign that had gone on since about 1860, won independence. Except for six counties in the north, the whole island of Ireland became a Republic in which, until about 1970, the Catholic church retained a lot of power.

The six counties in the north didn't join the rest of Ireland in 1922, because by then a big Protestant population had descended from the incomers of 1689 and the six counties remained 'Northern Ireland' - the fourth part of the United Kingdom. But nearly 300 years later, a lot of Catholics in the north felt oppressed by this. Protestants got the best education and jobs, owned the best land, and dominated local government. Many Catholics from Northern Ireland joined the IRA – the Irish Republican Army. The IRA were Nationalists who wanted the six counties to leave the United Kingdom and join the Irish Republic.

In the late 1960s the IRA began a terror campaign, which meant shooting and bombing in Northern Ireland, and on the British mainland. Many northern Irish Protestants, called Loyalists, opposed them with similar acts of terrorism. The violence went on for more than thirty years, and that time was called The Troubles. Whenever a bomb went off, one side or the other claimed responsibility.

British soldiers were stationed in Northern Ireland as a 'peacekeeping force' but the First Battalion, Parachute Regiment, killed 14 protestors on one notorious occasion in 1972 called Bloody Sunday. They were publicly condemned for this on the mainland. It came as a a huge shock, because this sort of thing was unheard-of in the British Isles. The last time the army had shot peaceful protestors anywhere in the United Kingdom had been in 1820; schoolchildren learned about it as a shameful historical event.

So Bloody Sunday, an occasion on which the Army got out of control, was certainly counter-productive and boosted the IRA's cause enormously, especially among people of the Irish diaspora in North America. The British Government were not doves. On the whole they were hawks. But after this, their army was discouraged by the legislature and judiciary from committing unnecessary acts of aggression. The soldiers concerned were eventually tried. They largely escaped punishment, although the present Prime Minister accepts that they were to blame and has issued an apology.

Would that happen in Algeria? I doubt it. The regimes of the Maghreb perceive all criticism as a threat.

Nor, in theory, do the British allow summary justice to result in death. It is true that during the Troubles both Loyalist and Nationalist paramilitaries were tried in Diplock Courts. This meant a suspension of the mainland British jury system. In Diplock courts people could be found guilty of terrorism and sentenced as criminals, rather than political prisoners. But there were trials, and due process, and no death sentences.

Margaret Thatcher was a hard-liner on Ireland. In the late '80s she misjudged public opinion by forbidding the BBC to broadcast the IRA leader's voice. You could watch him talking, but his words would be voiced by an actor. Viewers found this bizarre. The public expected the BBC to be impartial and this subservience to Thatcher made it lose face. The BBC responded that in the Second World War it had refused air-time to the Nazi enemy, and this IRA man was also an enemy, hostile to the British state. However many of the British public on the mainland, and the Irish in the Irish republic, remained apathetic. They didn't care who won as long as the shooting stopped.

I reported from Belfast several times in the early 1990s. When I turned my attention to Algeria, and making a programme about it, it was 1994 and - with Thatcher no longer Prime Minister - British politicians and the IRA were trying to negotiate a peace. In England, the BBC was back to normal and you heard both sides of an argument.

Algeria was different. Ordinary people were shot, or otherwise met violent deaths, but no group claimed responsibility. There was no accountability. People lived in dread because they didn't know where the enemy was - the military, one of the rival paramilitary outfits, who was it this time? State TV contributed to the confusion. It was the main source of news and you never saw the opposition, only whole-hearted support for the Army, who were matching the fundamentalists atrocity for atrocity.

As it turned out, these were the first years of the Blood Decade. But at the time, I was excited to hear that nearly all the Algerian leaders had agreed to put their sides of the argument to one another in conditions of cordiality, in Rome, in November '94. The régime refused to send a representative but at least the others would talk to each other. Their hosts would be from Sant'Egidio, the pacifist community of the Catholic Church in Rome, and the conference would be held at the ancient convent of Sant'Egidio after which the community was named.

For me, this was an extraordinary opportunity to catch voices the Algerian public hadn't heard, speaking in their own language. The opposition had never had a chance to put its case on State media but MBC could give them a hearing. I learned that about a dozen Algerians were going to speak at the peace conference over two days. We couldn't possibly broadcast the whole thing, so I put a proposal forward. I suggested to my News Editor that if I could get, say, half a dozen key speakers together for a round-table discussion, preferably in a room in the same building, we could make a good programme out of it.

He agreed, although to my dismay he wouldn't sanction more than one cameraman and a producer/director - an American, freelance at the time, who knew Arabic. I concocted a Plan B about the number of cameras, but first I had to see if Sant'Egidio would allow us to film there. They would, so I then invited every one of the participants to make time to appear on MBC. Most of them accepted willingly.

Sant'Egidio is three hundred years old. I'd seen the beautiful room where we'd asked them to come for the shoot at the end of the first day's conference, and I knew that one camera wasn't going to be enough. We'd need decent lighting, three cameras and a live edit by the American guy; it wasn't as if you could ask the distinguished Algerians to 'Just do that again, would you?' So we put Plan B into action: we went ahead and booked local crews to supplement the cameraman from London.

In the morning we were able to get some wide shots of the start of the conference itself before the participants went into closed session. Several of the speakers, including Ben Bella himself, spoke fluent Italian. One, who had come from Switzerland, spoke English with an American accent. And of course, as educated Algerians, they all spoke French. One of their hosts admitted that he was surprised to meet such urbane, cultured men. Algerian freedom fighters had a wild image. 'You're such an intelligent bunch,' he said 'I'm sure you'll be able to find a middle ground.'

MBC shot the round-table session on the first evening. The only notable who didn't come was Louisa Hanoune, the communist leader. Ben Bella was there. He had been the most famous of the Algerian revolutionaries during the war of independence in the fifties and sixties, but had been under house arrest from about 1965 for many years, until he went into exile around 1980. In subsequent years he had kept a low profile, so it would be the first time Arab viewers had seen him in decades. He was in his 80s: tall, elegant, healthy and sharp as a whip. He'd told me 'I'll do it because you're an Algerian. Not because you represent MBC.' He knew MBC was Saudi owned and he didn't like the Sauds.

We had Anwar Haddam, from FIS, the Islamic Salvation Front which had won the election in '91 but had been denied the right to take office. He was a nuclear physicist who had been living under protection in America. Abdelhamid Mehri came, from FLN (the National Liberation Front) which had essentially driven out the French and was thought by many to operate as the political wing of the Army. Several others took part including Sheikh Mahfoud Nahnah, from Hamas. This was a chance for viewers to see exactly where all these opposition leaders stood on the spectrum of opinion.

My main aim was to find out why, in their opinion, so many people were dying violent deaths. I began by asking Ben Bella - how d'you see Algerian politics today?

He said it was like a relay race. It didn't matter who happens to be winning at a given time, the same old faces kept coming around.

He prefaced that pointed remark, as they all did, with the formalities; *In the name of Allah the most merciful and compassionate, gratitude for giving us the wonderful country of Algeria.* They all spoke at length. I was prepared for this; more sophisticated politicians would have spoken fast and to the point for television, but I knew I wouldn't get sound-bites. Frankly the message, on this occasion, was more important than the demands of the medium.

They'd been talking for only a few minutes when somebody pointed out that according to the principle of Shura, decisions should not be made without consulting those who would be affected by it, and this violence was affecting ordinary citizens, who were paying the price for the internecine squabbles of their own parties, as well as the brutal Army. The Hamas guy was exasperated. Haddam from FIS said it was their fault for starting the violence. I could see a spiral beginning, a tit-for-tat of *you did this*, but *you did that and it was worse*, and *how about what you did when...*

Algerian history is even more complicated than that of Northern Ireland but I managed to prevent a fist fight by playing Devil's Advocate, to deflect aggression. I put the régime's point of view. Nobody came to blows. They all had their say, and although some of them spent a lot of time blaming other people, there was broad agreement about what the issues were.

We recorded two hours and ten minutes - forty minutes too much. We had to cut it. While I was in the edit suite back in London I got a call from the Algerian Ambassador. I knew him slightly, from having met him at official functions.

'Hacene I've been asked if you'd do me a great favour.'

'If I can, of course.'

'I believe the Islamic Front were represented at the Sant'Egidio Conference recently.'

'Yes.'

'And you've made a programme that features them.'

'Among others, yes. We made a round-table programme and they took part.'

'Well I'd be very grateful if the Islamic Salvation Front could be deleted.'

'Deleted?'

'Yes. I'm asking you to cut out whatever it was that Haddam or his acolytes had to say.'

'I can't do that.'

'It's for the sake of national security, Hacene.'

'I'm sorry, Your Excellency. This isn't the way we work here. MBC isn't under Algerian control.'

He sighed. 'Well. I have done my best. I was asked to make the request, and I'm sorry you feel you can't concede on this.'

The Sant'Egidio Conference itself was extremely constructive. Months later it resulted in a document, a formal set of proposals, approved by all the participants, that were put before the régime for negotiation. The régime didn't want to know, but it was, at least, a start: the opposition had a coherent position.

Our programme aired, within days of the event, at nine o'clock one Saturday night. One pro-régime Algerian newspaper was particularly dismissive, and singled me out as 'probably a cousin of the terrorist'. (I do share a surname with a rebel leader but then, so do a lot of people.) The day after transmission, one of the participants - a man called Boukrouh - called a Press Conference. He was angry. I'd deliberately cut his contribution, he said. I'd distorted his whole argument and MBC was not to be trusted to tell the truth

I was summoned to my senior manager's office and I played both tapes, the original at 130 minutes, and the ninety-minute version we'd put out. All I'd cut was this man's ramblings about history which the audience knew anyway, and some clips from other people where they'd mumbled or repeated themselves. We agreed that all I'd done was a regular, unbiased edit, but I should write to Boukrouh anyway to explain the requirements of a TV schedule. I did that, in detail, in Arabic, but he remained aggrieved.

I had in fact made a useful programme. The expatriate community were particularly pleased as they had been starved of unbiased news about Algeria. The BBC's Listening Service put out a monthly digest of the most significant political broadcasts world-wide, and a transcript of key points was included in that. This was extracted for circulation within the Foreign Office and to Downing Street, with a note on it emphasising that it must be read by anyone who wanted to understand what the issues in Algeria were, and who was saying what.

And then, to my surprise, MBC was invited by Algerian State TV to make a programme for them, using their own crew. It would be along 'whither Algeria?' lines. I hadn't spent any time with my family for years, so I seized the chance.

We made a documentary called 'Who's killing whom in Algeria?' that explained the nature of the conflict and interviewed religious leaders and ordinary people. One old couple made a particularly strong impression. The old lady was crying, and beside her, her husband was saying

'If my son had died fighting against foreign invaders I would be proud. If my son died in an accident, I would say God had willed it. But my son was killed by Algerians and I don't know who they are!'

Their son had been a policeman.

The programme was well received in London. And then I got a call from the head of the Algerian military's press bureau.

'You're a journalist! You've been all over the world! What d'you mean by asking such a question - who's killing whom? You know exactly who's killing whom.'

'No I don't. You heard that old man we recorded. Even he doesn't know who killed his son, so how would I?'

'It's terrorists! You know that.'

'No. There are a lot of unexplained killings. A lot of people say it's the army.'

'Rubbish. You know it's not and you should say so.'

'I know nothing of the kind.'

'Well, take it from me. It's terrorists.'

'You have no evidence of that. You think I should say what you want me to say?'

'Yes. That is your duty.'

'If you think that, you don't know what journalism is.'

State television simply refused to broadcast it.

As for Boukrouh - when he stood at the next presidential election, we interviewed every candidate but him. MBC refused to show him. He rang me, furious, complaining of MBC's alleged bias and bitterly recalling that I'd cut some of his contribution to the Sant'Egidio programme. I explained yet again that TV gets edited. I don't think he got it. He felt disrespected. I was dealing with a man who for some reason believed that we had a duty to broadcast his every word. We didn't.

This kind of thing happens time and again with the régimes: they do not understand the concept of neutrality in the media, and they spend a lot of public money spying on the opinions of harmless individuals who don't even have a public platform.

Western politicians are far more media-savvy. They understand our time pressures. They know that the shorter and snappier the sound-bite, the more chance they have of getting on air. And they understand that we do have power to exclude. We would never exclude a person because of what they say, but we might well do so because they're known to be disruptive. We work to a tight schedule at all times. We want people who turn up, say what they want to, and go. We don't offer them editorial control.

In the United Kingdom you can broadcast anything, short of personal slander, offensive racial or sexual prejudice, or physical threat. A Member of Parliament has published a book suggesting that British Military Intelligence operatives concealed the truth about a politically significant death related to the Iraq invasion in 2003 – because it was in fact murder, in the interests of the British and Americans. Nobody's jailed him. You can buy that book anywhere, and the MP is now a Government minister, because after all, he is entitled to voice his opinion and he doesn't accuse any individuals. If you broadcast an unpopular opinion you don't get a call from the Foreign Office or the Ministry of Defence. They may get angry, they may try to undermine you, but unless national security is directly threatened or the laws against personal harassment are broken, they have to put up with it. In Britain it is difficult to prevent transmission altogether, even if your programme isn't simply expressing opinion, but revealing facts that may endanger life. The Ministry might first have to prove to a Judge that there is a dangerous risk to national security. (And these days, the Ministry would be too late anyway, as we know from the revelations of Edward Snowden and Bradley Manning.)

Freedom of speech should, I believe, be the goal of all Arab media. There is an information vacuum in that world, and nature abhors a vacuum. All kinds of lies and half-truths become current when nobody knows whom they can trust.

As a journalist, I try hard to be neutral. As an individual, I admit that I am angry about the dreadful state in which the Palestinians have to live. I've been to Israel many times and have been well treated by Israelis and Jews generally, but I cannot believe the Palestinians will ever have decent lives while Netanyahu is in power. I've interviewed him and I believe he and his supporters will be brutal adversaries to the end.

I first went there in the early 90s when peace had temporarily broken out. I arrived at Ben Gurion airport, and the lady at Passport Control took my British passport, flicked through it and said

'Where are you from originally?'

'Algeria.'

'You go to a lot of Arab countries. Are you sure you want me to stamp this?'

'Yes,' I said. 'I'm media, we can go anywhere.'

'It'll create problems for you, you know that?'

'I'll live with it.'

The producer and I went to the Foreign Press Office on our first day there, had our pictures taken and got our plastic foreign-media cards to show at checkpoints, or with curious police, whatever. It was all routine stuff.

The woman at Passport Control had been right that I'd have problems when I left Israel for other Middle Eastern countries, but I was looking for an opportunity to make the point: journalists don't take sides. Well, I certainly got it. I was stopped on my way into the Emirates soon afterwards. And then when I entered Lebanon, the official looked up and said

'You've been to Israel.'

'I have.'

'Why? Why did you go there?'

'I'm a journalist.'

'You're a journalist so you take that risk? Why? What were you doing in Israel?'

'Listen,' I said 'Your politicians are talking to Israelis, sipping beer and whisky every night, and you challenge me? I'm just a journalist. It's my job to show what's going on. I need to go through that airport. It has nothing to do with taking risks.'

I had made the point. And if I have the opportunity, that's what I always will do.

Chapter 8

Opportunities

If you're sent out to report on a horse-race or a flower show, and something more newsworthy happens while you're there, you drop everything and go for it.

I first found this out in Israel. When I went there for the first time, in '92, Rabin and Arafat had begun talks and the shooting had stopped. We made a documentary about possible obstacles to peace on both sides. We filmed the hard-line settlers, Palestinians of the diaspora who were returning as an entrepreneur class, Israeli employers who liked having cheap labour, and other Palestinians – still in the camps after decades of deprivation and injustice – who, since the truce, hadn't been able to cross into Israel to get work. It was a desperately complex situation and I interviewed significant people, like Shimon Peres. The documentary we made was nuanced and subtle I think; not negative but hopeful.

I went to Israel for a second time in '95 to make a documentary about the Oslo Accords, the peace signed off by Arafat and Rabin. I had a crew from our Jerusalem studio. Rabin had made concessions - the border was open, Palestinians could find work, and the Israelis could shop cheaply in Palestine. However there were people in Israel who refused to concede that Israel should ever be inclusive. They did not want peace.

An increase in terrorism was the result. Hamas was increasingly using suicide bombers to blow up buses and drive bomb-laden trucks into cities and so was Islamic Jihad. We drove to Ashkelon and then out to Gaza, where a couple of Israeli soldiers had recently been killed and there had been a major attack that year on a bus full of soldiers. We interviewed people, did some filming and came back to send our footage. I sent the story to London from our office, went back to my hotel and turned on the TV. Something was happening - a crowd in the open air lit by arc-lights, panicky shots of policemen shouting, ambulances, sirens – but I did not understand Hebrew. What was all this? I picked up the phone and and rang the local MBC bureau chief.

'I just turned the TV on. Has something happened?'

'Yes,' he said, 'it's Rabin. He's been shot at a rally in Tel Aviv and taken to hospital. I was trying to get hold of you. MBC wants you to go live.'

He couldn't come into the office himself, because he lived in the West Bank and the curfew had begun. 'But,' he said, 'we've got David, he's a Jewish guy, a cameraman. Get yourself down there, and I'll get him to come and open the office. He can set up to record you and get you a live feed to London.'

'I don't know what happened though.'

'No but you can take some notes from me. Have you got a pen?'

'Just a minute. Yes.'

'This is the information I have.' So I took notes and when I went live I explained that at the end of the rally Rabin had been shot at several times and it looked serious. One of his guards had been injured. An ambulance had raced away with Rabin, and a man had been arrested. As I talked they were showing agency shots of the crowds, the ambulance, his wife Leah and so on - and even the assassination itself. The whole world was now looking at Israel; and within minutes news arrived that Rabin had died. His widow was bitter about the ultra-nationalists of Netanyahu's Likud, and probably she already knew - as the public did not - that the assassin himself was one of them. They were determined to wrest power from Rabin and his supporters.

In the morning the Israeli papers noted that MBC had been the first Arab channel to report the assassination. Rabin's funeral was to take place at Mount Herzl that day, and the documentary was put on hold as Heads of State, senators, former Heads of State and Foreign Ministers were arriving from all over the world. They included President Mubarak of Egypt, the President of the European Council Felipe Gonzalez, and Boutros Boutros-Ghali who was UN Secretary-General at the time. President Clinton and the King of Jordan would be among many to deliver eulogies. Our crew were inside the King David Hotel with all the Israeli media, getting soundbites from all these people if they could. I doorstepped King Hussein and he spoke about what Rabin had achieved, and what the obstacles to peace might be.

The whole day opened my mind to just how many angles to achieving peace there could be; some I had never even known or considered, and I don't think many others had either. I got a lot of information from listening to other journalists.

I stood among the crowds surrounding Rabin's coffin draped in the blue and white flag, talking to camera in Arabic. I said how remarkable it was that this man, who had urged Israelis to break Palestinians' bones during the first Intifada, had signed a peace agreement with them. Israelis all around me could hear this and some understood it perfectly well. 'What d'you mean by saying that?' one of them said. 'He never threatened to break anybody's bones.' What I saw was an Israeli who spoke Arabic, so I got an interview with him. You have to take advantage of the moment and give hecklers a voice.

Well, usually. Pieces to camera are perilous. All over the world, in towns where nothing else is going on, you get small boys pulling faces behind you, middle-aged men crowding around grinning at the camera, or – if the crowd is hostile - people shouting and putting their hands over the lens. You generally rely on your producer to get rid of them politely, but everybody's human, and once I was driven over the edge. It was in '92 when I first went to Israel and we drove out to a notoriously troubled area with about 400 settlers. We talked to Palestinian children who said it was hard to get to school because often their way was blocked by settlers, and the Israeli soldiers who were supposed to implement the peace did nothing. Simply by being there, I could tell that the settlers controlled the situation. The cameraman indicated one of them while he was setting up. She was about forty, wearing spectacles, just standing around.

'We might have trouble with that one,' he muttered. 'I've seen her before.'

I began my piece to camera, pointing out in Arabic that although there was a truce these settlers were still doing their best to disrupt it. The bespectacled woman, dressed as all the Orthodox women were in calf-length skirt, sensible shoes and big headscarf tied at the nape of her neck, started pulling at the cameraman's arm and shoving the camera. I stopped talking. The camera was working, and filming. I walked towards her and spoke in English.

In Najaf - Iraq in 2003

'We are doing a story. Do you understand English?' I pushed her away from the camera, hard - she staggered backwards, looking shocked. 'You are not allowed to touch the camera. Go away. We're accredited journalists and we're working.'

A couple of soldiers approached. 'Have you finished?' I looked at the cameraman.

'It's fine, I got most of it before she started.'

'You'd better leave,' the soldier said. 'Come with us. That woman can make things difficult here. We know her. We'll take you.'

'It's OK,' I said. 'We'll use our car but if you want to lead us out that's fine.'

We drove off, rather shaken because we'd been at a volatile location where Israeli extremists and Palestinian extremists could clash at any moment. Asking myself, later, whether I could have turned the situation to advantage –I don't think so. That woman was not a person who would have made any rational comment on camera, because she simply didn't concede our right to be there at all.

Crowds of listeners are perilous. Twice, when I was in Najaf in Iraq, the same sort of situation arose. Najaf is the Shi'a holy city, full of pilgrims to the tomb of the Caliph Ali (Ali Ibn Ali Talib, the Prophet's son-in-law). Shi'as revere Ali as the first among those Caliphs who followed Mohammed, a Prophet; Sunnis esteem him but not so highly. For Shi'as it is therefore necessary to say *Peace be Upon Him* as you would after the name of Mohammed.

'As you know,' I was saying to camera, there are many visitors to the tomb of Ali and they come from all over the world.' I didn't say the reverent words afterwards, as a Shi'a would have done, and one of them jumped in front of me and shouted

'You did not say Peace be Upon Him!'

'I understand that sir, but I am Sunni. We say it only for Prophets.'

'You are here in Najaf! The Shi'a city! You should say it.' He ambled off grumbling.

The Middle East is not like working in the West. It's a place where you often meet with hair-trigger volatility about politics and religion. Opinions are rigid, so if your words transgress local convention in any way, they don't see you as a person doing a job that demands a cold impartial eye; they see you expressing a view for which you, not your channel or your co-religionists, must take responsibility. It's personal. Reaction is immediate and unthinking and can be violent. In Saudi Arabia or Bagdad it's the same; if people see something they dislike, they attack it. You can be a journalist talking about the Prime Minister or standing next to a tomb talking about the deceased – imply any allegiance, voice any opinion, and somebody will verbally or physically attack you. Above all, you can never afford to lose your temper.

Chapter 9

Learning from the old school

I had done a good job with the Algerian leaders, but a 90-minute round table discussion might not be given air time today. Certainly not in the west, where an issue-led political discussion might last 45 minutes at best and would probably take place in front of a vociferous audience, with messages coming in online. There would be more conflict and public participation and less deference.

Producers in the Arab world think that the audience has learned to expect constant excitement from the screen. It's true that talking heads can be dull. They demand close attention, yet the picture and setting can be a distraction rather than a help. In some ways, radio is the better medium for conveying ideas.

Given only one interviewee (rather than six people with conflicting opinions), I find I can get most people to be concise, but Arabic is flowery. As the questioner, you have to make the boundaries of the answer absolutely clear: to maintain control, in other words. Tim Sebastian, the ITN news man, told me that in 1989, with Poland recently liberated from Russian domination, he was sent to Warsaw to interview their new Finance Minister. It was his first assignment and when he came back, the News Editor watched his footage with his head in his hands. 'Don't ever do that again,' he warned. Tim had allowed the Minister to dominate the interview, and of course he'd talked on and on, straight to the camera like a Head of State giving an address to the nation. Sometimes you have to interrupt - summing up what they're trying to say, and moving on. 'So you believe the demonstrators are brainwashed by foreigners. What's your proof of that?'

That's an open question. They have to come up with a response that adds something. They can't say Yes or No.

You can run an interview into a wall by asking closed questions. There is a famous radio news extract from the 1960s which the BBC used to use for training purposes. The luckless reporter had doorstepped an African politician, and the recording ran something like this:

Good morning Prime Minister.

Hmph.

I'm John Smith from the BBC. Did you find the conference productive?

No.

Did you feel that Mr Y's position had any validity?

No.

Was there any point you might have conceded?

No.

Did you think Mrs J might change her mind?

No.

Aren't you worried about the outcome of these entrenched positions?

No.

Prime Minister, do you not wish to talk about the conference at all?

Hacene Zitouni

No.

So you intend to stay silent?

No comment.

Do you believe in telling people what you think?

No.

I was beyond such elementary mistakes by the time I met Sandy Gall, but I still had a lot to learn. He'd worked for Reuters since 1953 and for ITN as a Foreign Correspondent and presenter for decades. His work in Afghanistan in the 80s, when it was still under Russian occupation, had been nominated for awards; to make his documentaries, he'd lived with the mujahideen fighters for months on end throughout the Soviet-Afghan war. He had written books about the situation there, and he and his wife had started a charity for landmine victims which the family still ran.

When his unusually perceptive documentaries and books appeared, British military intelligence were more than interested. At least once on his return to Britain from Afghanistan, they invited him to a very good lunch and, in their charming and polite way, debriefed him. In other words, they picked his brains for even more detail about the thinking of different mujahideen groups. (He revealed this himself, later, in a book.) He was, in fact, providing MI6 with the kind of information about the Afghan warlords' opinions that I had openly given them in my programme about the Algerian opposition.

Because he'd done this, when his book came out, some reviewers wondered whether he'd been more than a journalist; had he in fact been an MI6 operative, manipulating his contacts in Afghanistan in favour of the west? It seems not. Two investigative journalists co-wrote a book about the line that journalists walk between truth-telling and betrayal. They scrutinised his career closely and concluded that yes, Sandy Gall was just a reporter with a passion for the truth.

Afghanistan was his great project, but by 1995 he'd retired. He was still fit and avidly following events in the civil war there. After the Soviet defeat, the warring groups of mujahideen were well supplied with ex-Russian armaments and the internal conflict showed no sign of ending.

He was impatient to put certain points about Afghanistan and how the west should approach it. He declared his interest to MBC, and suggested a documentary would be timely. The Taliban, who were at the time occupying Kandahar, were gathering in a thirty-mile radius around Kabul, and threatening to take it. MBC agreed on one condition: that he take an MBC reporter there to train him in war reporting.

This was a terrific opportunity for me. I set off with him and the cameraman he always worked with, a British guy called Simon. With Sandy Gall, I learned something just about every day.

The first thing was how to obtain bodily comforts in a war-torn city under sporadic fire, while at the same time networking and figuring out original angles on all your stories. I'd never been to Kabul before, and found a strange mix of coffee-coloured mud-brick mansions and low modern buildings on a wide plain with a muddy riverbed straggling through it. Twenty miles away, a grey-brown range of mountains rose along the horizon. Many of the buildings had been bashed about by fighting and stood in a state of disrepair, but the streets were busy with Central Asian people of two or three distinct types. Flocks of small local women presented an odd silhouette, in pleated pale blue burqas that covered them entirely, with lacy slits in the headpiece through which even the eyes were invisible.

Sandy Gall told me he usually stayed at the German Club, but when we arrived the building was near-derelict. There was one person staying and two or three staff, who I suppose were living there without pay, for shelter. Fighting in the past year had been fierce, the Germans had left, and there was no money to maintain the place. It was filthy, and when you clicked a switch to find out just how filthy, you discovered there wasn't a light-bulb in the place.

The pool outside, which looked as if it had last been emptied around 1970, was an expanse of dark brownish-green, floating plastic rubbish and algae. Mournful-looking snakes occasionally rose from the depths to slide along beneath the surface before disappearing again.

We peered down.

'Can't this at least be cleaned?'

'We have no electricity, so the pump won't work.'

Somehow Sandy found a generator, an electrician with light bulbs, and some people to exterminate the cockroaches and smarten up a few rooms, and we moved in. The staff couldn't supply food, so we had to eat out. One morning I woke up to the sound of a cockerel crowing. I looked out of the window at a jumble of suburbs that stretched for miles across the plain. Tall delicate minarets needled the sky above the dome of a mosque.

Somebody sighed in the garden. Six metres below me, in the dark rubbish-strewn pool, a pale figure lay lazily afloat.

'My god! What are you doing?' I was horrified.

'I need my breakfast and I need my bath,' said Sandy. I suppose, when you lead a life of the kind he does, in which anything may happen from one moment to the next, the rituals of life - the glass of whisky in the evening, the morning dip - are a way of imposing order on chaos.

He brought life to the place. Within a week, the pump worked and the pool was emptied, thoroughly cleaned and refilled. He employed cooks. He invited people from western NGOs, local opinion-formers he happened to know, and journalists from everywhere. We had a big seating area in the garden, Afghan food and delicious fruit, and a car with a driver to take us wherever we needed to go. Of all the things I learned from him, I think resilience - his refusal to give up at the first hurdle - was the most important. For Sandy, however difficult the circumstances seemed at first sight, there was usually something you could do to adapt them to suit you.

One week after our arrival, the MBC team at the German Club were the social hub of Kabul. Sandy knew most people, and the ones he didn't, knew him. I was awestruck. He was a legend in his own lifetime, and a person who got things done, rather than waiting for somebody to do it for him. The food and drink and laughter around the pool were for a purpose. He was soaking up information from everybody he met, and information is our stock in trade. He mentally registered every useful fact about who knew what, who disliked whom, and who might be able to help him get at the stories he wanted.

He wasn't ever reckless and he judged people and situations well, I think. Over the fourteen years of war with the Soviet Union, he had become friendly with Ahmad Shah Massoud. This man was so brave a fighter that he was called the Lion of Panjshir. He loathed the Taliban. He and Sandy shared a mutual liking and deep respect for one another; they had been through a lot together. Sandy, who was much older, was a veteran of war reporting from the Hungarian uprising of 1956 to the Vietnam War and had lived with Massoud and his mujahidin on and off throughout the years of the insurgency.

Later on, when Massoud and his followers finally retreated from Kabul to maintain resistance to the Taliban with the Northern Alliance, news media would give the impression that 'warlords' - as the leaders of the Northern Alliance were called - were piratical, bloodthirsty fellows who understood little other than guerilla fighting. Ahmad Shah Massoud wasn't like that at all. He disliked violence, and appreciated the value of compromise. The more thoughtful western journalists recognised this in him. In '96 one of them called him 'the only man standing between Afghanistan and future Taliban massacres.'

Sandy introduced me to Massoud and we communicated in French. He was tall, rake-thin, and smiling, and serving at the time as Minister of Defence. He had been educated in French, at the Lycée in Kabul which had - until the Russians came - been the Afghani Eton. He spent years living rough with his men, and was a brilliant leader who could communicate with all kinds of Afghan, and even his enemies, in Pashtun, Urdu or Farsi. They respected him as a military leader, and an engineer - he had studied at Kabul University.

And then (because there are at least two sides to every question) with the Taliban actively trying to take Kabul, we interviewed a Taliban leader. Sandy set that up, too. He did his interview in English; I did mine in Arabic. The Taliban representative spoke both.

Sandy's persistent preoccupation was with the cruel aftermath of the Russian retreat. Afghanistan is a beautiful country with naturally hospitable people. Its terrain varies from mountain to desert to lush fertile valleys. The Russians had sown it with over ten million concealed land-mines and the mujahideen had - on a smaller scale - mined areas around Soviet command posts. (Since 1997 most countries have banned their use.) There was no map to show where mines were. The charity Sandy had set up was dedicated to providing prosthetic limbs for the men, women and children disfigured by these vile weapons. Throughout the year, the wastes of central Afghanistan are criss-crossed by nomadic tribes, colourfully dressed travellers who pitch black tents in one place to graze their animals for a few months, and move on. Their children, golden-skinned, blond-streaked toddlers playing in the dirt, were usually the ones who lost legs, arms and eyes to land-mines.

Sandy used his land-mine report as an exercise for me to learn from. He already knew, through his charity, which hospitals we could film in. He told me

'There's not much point in doing a piece that just says "Look at this - it's terrible". We need an angle. We agree it's terrible but how can it be made better? Do they need more surgeons to work here? How can this country afford to give out prosthetic limbs? What's the situation with antisepsis? How can the Russian army be made to supply their maps? Is anybody trying to get mines banned? That sort of thing. If you're lucky you'll find the perfect angle as you work.'

He instructed me first to do the research. What was the scale of the problem? What was the background? We knew that. Most of these things were not IEDs (improvised explosive devices) but land-mines laid by an army; and there was plenty of library footage of the Afghan-Soviet war. What was the latest news? Who were the key individuals who knew most about it? What could we film? Might any of these people have an axe to grind - might they need balancing with a different opinion?

That was particularly important, since rumour had it that Saudi Arabia, whose rulers owned MBC, were backing extreme Islamists here. We didn't want anyone to suggest that we were supportive of militant Islam but nor did we want to show bias in another direction. We'd heard that a certain NGO (non-governmental organisation) had recently found mines in a particular location. I had to contact them and explain who MBC were, what we wanted to do and what the broadcast would do for them. They didn't have a press officer in Kabul, but they were willing to talk to us when I explained the global reach of MBC and how Sandy Gall was making a programme that would highlight the mines issue.

I went to see them. I explained that we'd like to interview them; I asked them if they could find a mine clearance officer who might be willing to talk on camera; and I asked them to describe how the clearance would take place – how they identified the precise location of the mine, and how it would be defused. I got them talking, I got them involved, and then I asked if we could follow them for a day with the camera.

Throughout this I was, as Sandy urged that I must, building a contacts list. I was beginning to see how he attracted so many people to the German Club.

We went out for a day to film a mine clearance. First, Simon shot general views: daily life. We were a few miles from Kabul on stony lane that led to a village. By chance, a man came along, driving half a dozen goats. Simon filmed him. We could use these shots later as cutaways. A woman from the NGO was interviewed, with the possible mine site in the background.

'The thing is, it's easy to build up a false sense of security,' she said. 'You walk along a path and you think it's safe because goats have been there before you. But you're heavier than a goat. A running child is more likely to hit the ground with his full weight on one foot than a goat is, so a child can detonate a mine that's been live and unnoticed for months. Herders sometimes miss concealed ordnance by inches.'

There was a genuine, live mine to be cleared. When well-financed armies do this, they use massive tank-like vehicles with heavy iron flails, like giant bike chains, whirring around and thwacking the ground. This was an NGO with a small budget. An ex-sapper, a mine-detection operative contracted to work at a high day rate, had to do it. Simon wore a harness to steady his camera and had to follow precisely in the man's footsteps. He dared not step an inch out of line.

The operative stepped gingerly along a track. He was clad in body armour and a helmet and mask and slung about with equipment, most noticeably a back-pack connected to a metal-detecting plate on the end of a pole. The pole was tucked under his right arm and as he trod slowly forward he swung it in an even arc just inches above the ground. At one point it set off a whining sound.

As soon as Simon heard that he stepped calmly back to us. And beyond. We all had to get further away, quickly. Simon then zoomed in to show what the man was now doing. This was just one mine, and it had to be detonated using explosive. The bomb disposal man put down a marker, tiptoed a pace or two back, lay on his stomach and placed an explosive charge at the site. He rapidly wriggled away, got to a safe distance and and detonated it.

The bang, shower of stones and dust, and the black smoke, were filmed. Simon's tracking shot behind the de-miner's approach was good too. Everything else would now have to be re-enacted. For instance, Sandy and Simon wanted shots from ahead and to the side of the now-harmless mine, so that viewer would see the metal-detector approaching head on. But Simon couldn't stand in the right place to get the shot until everything within a two-metre radius of the mine site had been checked. We watched the operative swinging the detector cautiously, methodically in wide semi-circles as he took tiny steps forward. Finally he said 'You can stand right there in front of the wall, and I'll do the walk I did before. Don't for God's sake go any further to your right or get behind the wall, okay?'

'Yup.' Simon knelt over the camera on the ground to take close-ups of the operative's hands as he pretended to lay an explosive charge. All this was new to me. I recognised that artifice was sometimes the only way to tell a story. This wasn't artifice of the cheating kind; it was in a good cause.

I interviewed the contractor. How much easier would his job be if people like him had accurate location records?

'If somebody gave us those tomorrow, best guess is about fourteen years. But without the plans I'd say twenty-five years at least. There'll be a lot more amputees by then.'

We were a small crew, with Simon taking the sound - including the explosion - on camera, and me interviewing with a mic connected by a cable. Sandy and Simon recorded scores of tapes because they were making a documentary, but I had to deliver short daily reports to MBC for the news. I did a quick piece to camera on the mines issue and we cut together some of Simon's shots. In voice-over I explained the delicacy of the work these ex-military contractors were doing and how long it took.

For my news reports, as well as Sandy's documentary, we filmed casualties in the hospital; little children, blinded or with stumps for limbs. I interviewed doctors. I interviewed Afghans about their lives, their culture and their politics. And all this was thanks to Sandy Gall's contact book. The mujahidin who would follow Ahmad Shah Massoud to the ends of the earth felt much the same about Sandy. He had lived with them in the Panjshir in their hardest times, and eaten with them, and now, in his sixties, he was their unofficial ambassador. He loved their country, and people loved him back.

In the spring of 2001 Ahmad Shah Massoud, the Lion of Panjshir, made a speech to the European Parliament in Brussels. He said he had a message for George W Bush: if peace were not restored to Afghanistan very soon, and if Pakistan and Saudi Arabia and Osama Bin Laden were allowed to continue backing the Taliban, then the United States and other countries would themselves suffer.

Ahmad Shah Massoud, who had always been so media-friendly, was cruelly killed by a bomb hidden in a fake television camera two days before September 11, 2001.

Massoud was a man of integrity, unassuming and charming, and made me want to know more about Afghanistan. I have gone back many times.

There was another lion in Kabul; a famous one, Marjan. He had been in Kabul Zoo since 1976. He even had a partner, a lioness. I made an item about him and how he had lived through so much, seen so much suffering, and suffered, himself, from hunger and neglect. How ordinary Afghan people, here, were trapped and neglected just like him.

Months later, I returned to see Marjan and he was blind. It seemed that some fool had climbed into the cage for a bet, and touched the lioness. Marjan, as you would expect, mauled him. The following day three grenades were thrown at the lion. He was blinded and his jaw destroyed. There was world wide publicity about Marjan, and the other suffering animals in the Zoo, and vets and other trained staff flew in from many countries; but poor Marjan, who had seen so much, died in 2002 aged only 23. This magnificent animal had lived with more dignity than some people seemed capable of showing. People wept, and they wept not only for Marjan. He was a symbol of all who were powerless, and had suffered in silence.

One small concern illuminates a much bigger concern. As I was told on my very first assignment, war isn't just bang-bang. People always need reminding about the inintended consequences of war. It is about the pain of people who are never directly attacked, but who are deeply scarred by emotional hurt: the loss of their children, their livelihood, their parents, their education, their chances in life – and even the loss of a lion in the zoo.

If, as a reporter, you can make that point, you may do some good.

Also, be prepared to learn, however old you get. I'd done lots of reports before I met Jonathan. He was about eighty, and he was with us as director of foreign assignments. He and I were watching a live broadcast from Kabul when he said

'Hacene, can you be there soon?'

'Kabul...? How soon?'

'Tomorrow.'

'Yeah,' I said.

'Ok. I will arrange it.'

He booked me onto a flight to Islamabad that left London at midnight, gave me a bundle of money and said he'd be in touch before I left. I went home, packed my stuff, drove to Heathrow and checked in. I got a call from Jonathan.

'There's a UN flight to Kabul out of Islamabad at 6am.' He gave me the name of the contact I must find at Islamabad airport. 'The cameraman will meet you in Kabul. He's a Brit who lives there.'

'Zitouni?' the guy at Islamabad said when I met him. 'Yes. Jonathan told me to expect you.' I paid, and so did some other journalists, and at 6am we were on the flight.

One hour later we landed in Kabul. Ron Kennedy, a freelance cameraman, was waiting, complete with equipment and ready to work; and there was a car to drive us to Kunduz, the war zone, right away. All this Jonathan had arranged from London.

I already knew that other journalists were trained by the BBC in those ex-military-run places where you learn protective techniques. And here was

Ron, a freelance, complete with helmet, flak jacket, water purifying tabs, first aid kit – he told me he, too, had taken courses in what to do if you were injured or arrested or kidnapped; it had cost thousands but empowered him to some extent. Well over a decade into my career as a war correspondent, MBC had still not got around to me, or any of its journalists, on any courses that might protect us. All I had was blind faith, an ambition to compete with other channels, and a cameraman I could trust.

Later that day I was able to broadcast live from Kunduz and it was all thanks to Jonathan. He knew what Sandy Gall did - how to translate thought into action, fast. He had worked for all the big broadcast organisations. You felt you could go off into the unknown and he'd get you there and back. In fact he packed me safely off to Guantanamo Bay once - as a correspondent, of course.

I suggested it at an editorial meeting in 2002. US sources had confirmed that mujahideen were being shipped over to Guantanamo, a tiny US-run corner of Cuba and kept there for 'questioning'. Cost-wise, it would have made more sense to send somebody from Washington, but I was sent because my news editor said No, Hacene should go, he's been following the story; he's on top of it. In Washington, MBC staff under-estimated local interest I think.

So I found myself sitting with Jonathan while he joked on the phone to US army officers somewhere in Florida. I was astonished.

'How do you know these people?'

'Just leave me to it. I'll get you there. And Nimr too.' Nimr was our Lebanese cameraman. An hour later, as I passed his desk, he looked up and grinned.

'Got it. You're with the first group of Arab journalists allowed in.'

At the time neither of us knew that a Sudanese Al Jazeera cameraman had been 'allowed in' as a prisoner already (he would be there for six years before they let him out in 2008). However we sent in our credentials, which were approved after a few days. We then flew to Miami and assembled along with people from the BBC, CNN and Canadian broadcasting, among others. The Americans flew us all, via Roosevelt Roads naval and air base in Puerto Rico, to their base on Guantanamo, Cuba. This turned out to have the facilities of a suburban town and its own small media centre. There was family accommodation, lawns, cinemas, a mall full of cheap watches and clothes, and easy access to blue sea and white sand: everything clipped, hygienic and sunny. You could land there and think prison camp? What prison camp?

with cameraman Nemer Ghazal in Guantanamo
as a first Arab crew allowed in the Bay

The prison camp is a bit different - in the middle of barren scrubland, cut off from the world by metal barriers and rows and rows of barbed wire. It wouldn't be easy to leave, with the beady eyes of armed guards keeping you in their gunsights from the watchtowers. We were allowed to see the internees from a few hundred yards away. They were not hard to spot because each man wore a vivid orange jumpsuit and was escorted by two guards. It was pretty near impossible for a camera to focus on any of these distant moving subjects through the layers of wire.

Our visit was a US army charm offensive, although I think we all remained sceptical. We were being allowed to know what we were allowed to know.

At the time - it was one of the very first media visits - not only could we not interview prisoners, but we didn't even know who was in there. Their names were not being revealed. Questions were answered by carefully prepared military personnel at a press conference. The summary transfer of teenage prisoners from Kandahar or Pakistan, the payment of bounties for picking people off the street, and torture, were all rumoured before they were confirmed.

At the time, Rumsfeld and Bush were being accused in the press of abusing human rights and not respecting the Geneva Convention simply by imprisoning these people in unknown conditions, for unknown reasons, apparently without evidence, and for no stated duration. Ah, they said, but these people are terrorists (that is, criminals) not soldiers (that is, prisoners of war), so they are not subject to the UN Declaration or the Geneva Convention. And anyway, they said, Guantanamo is not US soil. (Technically, it has been leased from Cuba since 1903). Every objection was met by arguments that appeared to come from a Rumsfeld/Bush virtual reality, where places and people were legally defined and re-defined according to their whim of the moment. As a result a lot of airtime and newsprint was wasted in debate about whether, if a valid case could be made against any of these men, they should be tried in criminal or military courts, and where, and whether or not prisoners in Guantanamo Bay could be subject to US criminal law, and so on, and so on.

However, although Donald Rumsfeld and George W Bush thought they could say 'it will be so because we say so' everyone would stop asking annoying questions – this was not so. They lived in a different world from reasonable, decent people, and seemed astounded that non-Arab media were as vociferous on this topic as anyone.

The American media were interested in the Arab reaction to what their government was doing. There was a Lebanese correspondent from Washington who worked for Abu Dhabi TV, as well as me. The CNN people invited me to speak on CNN America so I checked with London and they gave consent. On CNN I expressed the unease that all liberal media were expressing about the way Rumsfeld and Bush were trying to have their cake and eat it too: either these people were prisoners of war or they were criminals, but either way, they still had to be charged and given a fair trial. They came under somebody's jurisdiction. The only positive thing I could find to say was that they were in a place of safety by comparison with Kabul. (At the time, I didn't know about the waterboarding, or the fact that some of them were under 18.)

But I was there. I'd followed the story from Afghanistan to Guantanamo. MBC had been able to inform its audience thanks to Sandy Gall and Jonathan, who knew what they were doing. When there was a shake-up of staff, with the deliberate intention of bringing more Arabs aboard, people like Jonathan were not replaced with experts.

Instead, we got a clueless bunch who never understood TV.

Chapter 10

Downturn and upturn

One day late in 1997 I found the usual copy of the MBC house journal on my desk. Idly I glanced at it. A headline on the front page drew my attention at once.

The documentary series *The War in Bosnia*, which MBC produced over three episodes, attracted a good deal of interest both from viewers and international bodies. MBC received many letters and phone calls praising the coverage for attempting to show all the different sides of the Bosnian conflict, by recording the action when and where it happened. Upon the request of the International Court of Justice in the Hague, MBC provided copies of the documentary programme to aid investigations into the cases of the war criminals [*sic*] of those accused of genocide and other atrocities conducted during the Bosnian war.

MBC has received a letter from the United Nations International Tribunal for the prosecution of those involved in serious violations of international humanitarian law, committed in the territory of the former Yugoslavia since 1991, thanking MBC for their co-operation in assisting MBC in their work. Such international recognition has made MBC a point of reference sought by popular and official agencies, particularly in Europe where MBC has a large audience.

My emotions, on reading this, were mixed. I'd made *The War in Bosnia*, from pitch to post-production, with the help of a great team and an excellent American editor, Stephen Hall. It was aired in three one-hour episodes. We'd cut library footage and maps together to explain the historical background to the immensely complex situation in the Balkans, the wars of the early 1990s, and the recent discovery of mass graves. We'd shot hours of video and interviews. I'd squatted in a malodorous field in Srebrenica while the camera zoomed in on human remains sticking out of the ground beside me. There was an arm, grey flecked with green, decomposed. We'd filmed Serbs and Bosnian Muslims sheltering in the same rooms in Sarajevo. We'd let pictures speak louder than words.

And - a small point, perhaps - we'd risked our lives to make a fair, authoritative programme.

And here was MBC - essentially MBC's middle management - congratulating itself. It's often been said that journalism is the first draft of history. These managers hadn't bothered to tell us that our programme was being used as, literally, history - that it was considered sufficiently reliable to be shown to participants at the International Court of Justice, or that the whole channel - thanks to our work - now prided itself on being seen as an international journal of record. Nobody had mentioned 'many letters and phone calls praising the coverage' to me. Only by pure chance had I even noticed the item in the magazine.

I resented that. We should have been given the credit due to us. Not to do so was bad management. Good managers encourage people. And I remembered when this sort of thing had happened before; the round-table programme from Sant'Egidio had been circulated to key opinion-formers in the British Government, but I'd found out about that by chance, too.

British managers said 'That was a good piece of work, Hacene' when it was. If it was routine workmanlike stuff they didn't say much, and I didn't expect them to, but there remained implicit confidence and respect in knowing that I could be relied on to turn in a decent report. If I spoiled an idea by doing it clumsily, I was asked to work out a better way. And feedback from the public was taken seriously: just how seriously, I knew - I'd translated the BBC's feedback for its British executives as a student, and these people had brought the same consciousness to MBC.

Reaction always led to improvement. The British managers, who knew how to make programmes, understood that a good TV programme results from lots of good choices, and choices are not made in a vacuum. In 2000 I took a Lebanese-American producer to Dearborn, Michigan, reported from the expatriate community there. We got a big crowd of Arabic-speaking locals together in a public hall for a televised debate on the Presidential election candidates. George W Bush was fighting for re-election against Al Gore, who had been Bill Clinton's Vice-President. The debate was lively and interesting, the background of these Arab-American families was explained through the Detroit automotive industry, and I got praised for the programme. Edwin Hart, the Head of News, showed his appreciation.

That wasn't always the case with the Arab executives. As the years went on, and senior levels at MBC were increasingly staffed by people from the Middle East, there was less feedback of any kind. If you don't get a reaction to creative work, you're floundering: working in a void. MBC's new managers didn't understand how we worked. Few had ever made a television programme, so they didn't understand the facilities or skills required.

One symptom of this was dithering. With news, you don't dither: you act, like Jonathan; you make a decision based on good judgement and press the Go button. News has to be new. Yet time and again, as a war reporter with the new Arab managers, I found myself arriving at some war-torn location when the conflict was already entrenched. This didn't make good viewing. If a TV station shows the commencement of a conflict, the issues - the basic lines being drawn - are right there. You can explain them and keep the audience with you, from one report to the next, as things change. If you go in later, and you've still got only two minutes in which to explain a situation, you're faced with unravelling a ball of wool.

If you think for more than five minutes about the media, you recognise that they don't just reflect opinion and report events; to a large extent, they construct them. Many remote conflicts do not loom large on anyone's news agenda because nobody's sent a team there. Others make world headlines because somebody did go, and publicise the conflict, and then the whole press pack descended.

Management problems began when MBC, after its first years of operation, began to run a kind of quota system. Executive staff from the Middle East and North Africa got jobs rather than westerners. On the face of it, that's a good policy, and their most senior Saudi executive was a film-maker who knew exactly what what he was doing. But on the whole, Arab societies are not socially mobile. People are favoured because of influence and background, rather than talent. Unfortunately, because well-connected people feel entitled to get the best jobs and usually do, they are not necessarily motivated to work hard or learn from the experience of others. For the wealthiest, a job is a meal-ticket - pretty much like welfare payments for the haute bourgeoisie.

I found this out myself, years later when I was asked to run a training programme for would-be reporters. My managers knew that it was necessary to get people to work with experienced reporters. It was the way I'd learned, and the way the BBC teach their staff. Off I went to Saudi Arabia, and started to hold classes.

Woody Allen once said 90% of success is about turning up. How right he was. I would say 'I want you here at 8am for a news conference - bring your own ideas. I'll pick the best and you'll shoot three two-minute pieces and edit them, ready for 1pm.' Which is pretty much what happens in a real TV programme.

Hardly anyone would be there at 8am. Some would roll in at 10.30. One guy usually turned up at 1pm, having risen from his bed in the late morning.

In this, you could see how the professional future of these people - all male, mostly in their twenties - had been disabled by over-indulgence. When they're five they announce 'I want a bicycle.' A bicycle is provided, and a servant to teach them how to ride it. When they're 20 it's 'I want a degree.' Somebody is paid to write their essays and theses. When they're 25 they decide 'I want to be on TV.' Then what? At a particular point in your life, you cannot find a servant to do the job. You have to learn it yourself. But you don't even know where to begin, because you have always been over-indulged.

This has come affected me personally. When the Algerian Ministry cut off my student grant and that of other poor boys, they kept on paying for the sons of the ruling élite to study abroad. Merit and effort should be rewarded, rather than connections, in this world.

Anyhow, of the twenty or thirty who had enrolled on the TV course, I found just two potential correspondents – one in Riyadh, and one in Jeddah. Both were competent although one wanted to be a producer, rather than appear on camera. The other, a thin clever chap who looked like a Yemeni rather than a Saudi, was so good that he got a job on TV in Dubai later - and on the 5th anniversary of the TV station, when he was asked how he began he said 'Hacene Zitouni trained me.' I was delighted.

I regretted that all the places on my course had not been offered to young people who were keen and motivated. Instead they went to the idle sons and cousins of well-connected people.

People who fail to do anything *except* turn up, and talk and produce paperwork, are destined – in the Arab media – to become managers. Among them are defensive people who are jealous of high achievers and undermine them, and arrogant individuals who think of programme-makers as worker ants. They have no idea how programmes are made and do not consider it their business to know. For them, it is a mechanical process rather like learning to cut out a suit or lay bricks: once you know the essentials, nothing changes much; there is a template into which everything fits. So as long as the workers are getting paid, they are expected to do as they are told on demand, like servants.

Attitudes such as those caused me to miss the birth of my son. The demands of the channel were relentless. Tanya, my English girlfriend, and I had discussed my long absences before we married in the late 90s. By then I had met enough divorced TV reporters to know that marriage to a foreign correspondent wouldn't be easy. All of them said the job had contributed to the breakdown of their marriage. An English manager at MBC had given me to understand that after five or six years as a correspondent I'd be offered a job as a presenter or maybe have a series; this was normal in bigger organisations because they understood the demands of family life. But when I did get the opportunity I was denied it, because the Arab managers protested that they should make the decision, and they didn't choose me.

The English executives had gone, now. At MBC, if you were told to join the press pack following the King of Saudi Arabia on an overseas visit to Asia, you went. There was no awareness that you might have a private life. Tanya gave birth to Atlas in Colchester Hospital when I was in Brunei. 'Oh, Hacene, you have a son now! That is good news.' But the travel remained relentless. In the first five years of my little boy's life I barely spent more than a couple of days in his company. Loyalty to an over-exacting employer can wreck a marriage. A certain amount of time apart refreshes a relationship, but too much can destroy it.

Such bad management of people was born of sheer ignorance. It was just one of many dysfunctions that were becoming evident in the late 1990s. Budgeting was hopeless; locations, and therefore costs and requirements, are hugely variable, and if production managers get it wrong and cut corners, they can put a whole team's safety at risk.

Also, employees expected the conditions and terms of employment that they would get in any well-run broadcasting organisation in Europe, but there was no competent Human Resources department with which to raise these matters. Staff ended up asking about sick pay or maternity leave in editorial meetings, and numerous tangential issues like this began to undermine our efficiency as a news-gathering channel.

For instance, the question of researchers - backup staff we didn't have. A single correspondent cannot have enough free hours in the day to keep abreast of events worldwide. If a senior CNN correspondent is suddenly called upon to report from a new place, he or she will be briefed. CNN employs people to get visas and book tickets, organise licences to film in the street, and provide carnets for the camera equipment, but if your operation is being run on a shoestring - which I began to feel it was, towards the end of the 90s - you and your team will have to do all this yourselves.

With Afghanistan, I had been lucky; thanks to Sandy Gall, I had a good grounding in the aims of the rival parties in Afghanistan and who was backing them. I have been able to follow Afghan events from Kabul and Kandahar to Guantanamo and beyond because successive editors, knowing that I'm likely to be up to speed already, can be confident in sending me to those stories. It's about building up research capital in your own mental information bank. You read the Arab papers as well as the major Western ones, and listen to news radio and watch current affairs television. You try to catch major documentaries like the one we made on Bosnia, and discussion programmes.

Small networks can be greatly disadvantaged if they lose their one and only expert on a major world conflict. It shouldn't, of course, happen that they only have one; they should always send at least two, to report from different sides of the argument. That's what the major networks do and it's politically healthy.

After the millenium, I was occasionally frustrated by opposition in the newsroom which seemed inexplicable. In June 2000 Britain was stunned by news of a terrible tragedy at Dover, the English Channel port. Customs officers made a routine check of a container lorry which had just arrived from Holland. It was stiflingly hot inside and they found 58 illegal Chinese immigrants dead of suffocation. One of the customs officers said she'd seen the Dutch driver sniggering as the pale thin bodies were discovered.

By ten in the morning a cameraman and I were in Dover. Many of the media pack were already there. We interviewed officials, and I did a piece to camera against the sea and the cliffs and the general outlines of Dover before we drove back. The piece was cut, assembled and ready for the news editor by 1.30pm - well in time to run on the 3pm bulletin.

This was a major event. It was topical since people-trafficking from poor places to rich ones was a cruel trade that benefited only criminals: in this case, Chinese Snakehead gangs. They profited from the open borders of Europe and the desperation of poverty-stricken people worldwide. It was of interest in every country. So when I watched the 3pm news and saw that the editor, an Iraqi, had used wire footage, not ours – I was incensed.

I confronted him immediately in the newsroom.

'Why didn't you use our piece?'

'It's my choice.'

'Was there anything wrong with it?'

'No. I just liked the Reuters stuff. It's my decision.'

'We drove all the way down to Dover, we interviewed people, we raced back here to cut it and you didn't bother to use it? Why? Was there something wrong with it?'

People were looking up from their screens.

'This has nothing to do with you. You don't decide what we put out, Hacene. *I* do.'

'You don't know your job.'

We had an American Head of News at the time, Edwin Hart. He came over. 'Hey you guys. Calm down. What's going on here?'

He listened to both sides of the story and turned to the editor.

'He got you the story. Why did you use wire footage?' The Iraqi rolled his eyes. 'What's wrong with Hacene's stuff?'

'I didn't look at it.'

'He gave it to you at 1.30 and you didn't even look at it? It's your job to look at what the correspondents bring in.'

'The Reuters stuff was fine.'

'But given the choice between agency material and something that's unique to us, you don't choose the agency. Is this personal? If so leave it outside. The news is more important than either of you. You're here to work.'

My story was aired at 6pm and at 9pm and at the following day's meeting there was a post mortem on the whole incident. It was made clear that editors must take what they're given - and at the very least, never withhold it without valid justification. I didn't even know the Iraqi guy; there was no personal issue. There are internal politics in most offices, and you'll always get people who demand minor changes simply in order to show they've got power. That's not worth worrying about. Unexplained rejection, though, should be dealt with by confrontation.

Some time after 9/11, I had a couple of good ideas turned down on cost grounds. 'Sorry, it's not a priority' started being heard at MBC. There were rumours of a move to Dubai. I was getting more and more discontented. What annoyed me more than anything was middle-management's passive-aggressive refusal to communicate. The indecision on the pilot programme was part of a pattern. These people didn't say No. They said maybe, we'll see, wait....They kept you hanging around and finally they made an excuse.

MBC was quite obviously not as brave or as well-functioning as it had once been, but I am optimistic by nature and I somehow imagined things would get better. I was on good terms with Ali, Sheikh Walid's right-hand man, and he usually managed to calm my anxiety about the way things were going.

Then the bombshell landed. In 2002 an announcement was made.

MBC would be split to become what they called a 'bouquet' of many TV channels with disparate programming (music, drama and so on). 24-hour news was to be handled by a new MBC channel called Al Arabiya, which would work out of a sparkling new media hub in Dubai.

A guy from Al Jazeera came to see me in London.

'You should be proud of your work,' he said. 'I say that, even though you made it for our rival.'

'We're not your rival,' I said. 'MBC is in London, and you're in Doha - it's different.'

'But they're opening a new channel and you'll be working in Dubai.'

'I won't. I'm staying in London with MBC.'

'I heard that. I couldn't believe it. Hacene, MBC left the news. You're a news man. You can't carry on with MBC.'

'Are you offering me a job?'

'Yes. Have you got any ideas?'

'Plenty.' I told him about a series idea I'd already put forward to MBC. I'd done a pilot for it and had nagged for months for a response only, finally, to be told 'there's no budget.' As a commissioning process, this was hopelessly unsatisfactory.

Mine was a simple enough idea, and I outlined it in a sentence or two.

'Coincidence!' he said. 'We have something like that. Why don't you take it over and do it?'

'I'd like to. But no. I've been working with MBC for a long time and the owners have never done me any harm. I'd feel bad if I let them down.'

'Oh come on. You know they're moving. This won't be their focus any more.'

'London will always be important. And I don't want to live in the Gulf. Sorry, but I'm staying.'

'Well, well. You're making a mistake. But I wish I could believe all our staff were as loyal as you.'

At the time I was satisfied that I'd done the right thing. I was working at MBC Battersea and I didn't see that changing. We were still a news channel, even if Al Arabiya began broadcasting from the Gulf. I had no intention of joining Al Arabiya. I was dismayed by the idea of moving to Dubai, but also by the changes to our own channel which I saw as a breaking of faith with the audience, and the staff. The channel I'd joined in '91 had been a beacon of hope, bravely showing the Arab world every shade of opinion. We'd interviewed the Israeli Prime Minister and he'd spoken Hebrew - the first event of its kind in the Arab world and one of many taboos we'd broken. I believed we could still regain some of that early glory.

But the seeds of Al Arabiya, and the end of MBC as a news channel, had been sown in 1996. That was when the débâcle with Orbit Communications led to the foundation of Al Jazeera in Doha. Al Jazeera, staffed as it was by BBC executives and producers, turned out to be very good. It attracted international recognition. It got scoops that the western channels couldn't, it showed members of the public saying what they really thought, and it had a reputation for fair reporting. Could MBC compete? Not any more. It had the production staff but executive decisions were being made late, and often wrong-headedly. Also it was in London, and the news these days was more likely than ever before to be in the Middle East. When you needed a senior reporter on the ground, the one who seized the opportunity at the shortest notice would get the prize.

Al Jazeera had made a land-grab for our territory and had succeeded.

What I did not grasp was that MBC, as a news channel, had never made a profit and with Al Jazeera as its competitor it probably never would. If it continued along its present path would eventually amount to no more than a hobby for Sheikh Walid, funded by the King. It needed major investment in staff and facilities and the Sheikh of Dubai, by making his media city and staff accommodation attractive and cheap, had offered an opportunity.

News alone could never deliver the kind of mass audience that advertisers wanted. To prosper and grow, Al Arabiya would require the kind of subsidy that only advertising revenue could supply.

Advisors looked at the books, and came up with a business plan. MBC Group must split into multiple channels aimed at distinct audiences; most of these channels would be entertainment based. Its news channel, the rival to Al Jazeera, would be based in Dubai. MBC's future in London, and mine, were uncertain.

Chapter 11

Crisis

I suppose I should have seen it coming. MBC made a second announcement. The London office would be shutting down, and moving to Dubai along with the rest of the Group.

I was shocked. I told Ali, whom I liked, that they wouldn't get good people to work in Dubai and anyway, the whole point was that if they were in London, they could broadcast whatever they liked. This would be different in the Gulf.

I was wasting my breath, because the decision had been made.

'Hacene, we've said. There's a job for you in Dubai.'

'No,' I said. 'If you want a correspondent in London, that's who I'll be. Otherwise I'll resign.' I had often reported from the Gulf and disliked the stifling heat.

'We don't need a correspondent in London. We're shutting this office down.'

'Okay. Then I resign.'

A week later they changed their minds. The Battersea office would stay open; I was still an employee. Life went on, although by the autumn of

2002 most people had left for Dubai and MBC's news bulletins were coming from there.

In September I sent an email to Dubai, where the decision-makers had already moved. I told them I would be sending footage of Bill Clinton, who would be the main guest at the Labour Party conference in Blackpool. We always covered British party conferences. I got feedback: *Sorry, not interested.* There were other, similar rejections. I had been used to having stories accepted, but they stopped signing my travel permits.

This seemed to me to herald a closing-down of something MBC had stood for, which was showing the wider world, not just the Arab world. I knew I wasn't losing my touch, but the direction had somehow changed when I wasn't looking.

'You seem to have forgotten what London is. What's going on?'

They wouldn't say. 'Al Arabiya's coming, with a new structure - you'll have to wait and see.'

I drew my salary, in Battersea, but I had nothing to do. I came up with ideas. Every time, I waited too long for a response and when it came it was 'there's no budget'. I began to feel that my non-job was wrecking my life – but I had a wife and child in England and brothers and sisters in Algeria to support. The burden was on me, as the oldest, to keep an income flowing in, so I hung around.

Finally came the announcement that Al Arabiya would transmit its first bulletin in February 2003 and most of their correspondents worldwide would be joining it. MBC would become MBC1, a family entertainment channel with hourly 5-minute bulletins but no extended news programming.

I resigned towards the end of 2002 and left.

Early in the new year, an Algerian businessman came to London to talk to me about a job. His name was Rafik Khalifa and he was in his thirties. He explained that he was about to start a new TV channel in London.

'Would you like to join us?'

'I'm interested, but I think we should put our cards on the table. May I ask you a question?'

'Go ahead.'

'Do you have any experience of running a TV station?'

'I'm a businessman. I have all sorts of interests.'

'I know, I've read the cuttings. You're very successful.'

He was. He had been all over the French and Algerian papers recently, and seemed to have appeared from nowhere. He owned an airline, a bank, desalination plants, a pharmaceutical company, entertained film stars at his parties in the South of France and kept a vast stable of Ferraris and Maseratis. That kind of conspicuous consumption doesn't necessarily indicate someone who's in it for the long haul. I wanted reassurance.

I went on. 'The thing is, I've been working for Saudis for ten years. Those people have a hard time emptying their pot of money as fast as it fills up. And even they have perceived a need to generate more funds than MBC costs to run. You're with me so far?'

'Yes.'

'So let me tell you about TV. It is a business where you count your gains and losses in seconds. Not days, or months, or years. If I call Reuters because I need some archive material from the Algerian war of independence, they will say How many seconds? In TV every second costs money. Right now MBC is still transmitting a full news three times a day, and a five minute bulletin on the hour every hour. The budget is sixty million dollars a year. Do you have that kind of money? And your channel is not just going to be news - you are talking a 24 hour channel of entertainment, drama, sport - that's hundreds of millions. *Do* you have that kind of money sir?'

'Money is not an issue. How much do you earn?'

I told him.

'Double it. What car do you drive?'

'A Mercedes.'

'Forget that. We'll give you whatever car you want. How do you travel? Business class?'

'Short distances, economy; longer, business.'

'You'll go first class, Hacene, short haul or long haul. Position: Head of International Operations for Khalifa Television.'

I told him to give me a day to think about it.

I was tempted. Still a little doubtful - I had been sincere in my concerns about the funding for an ambitious project like this - but my brother Kader encouraged me. He was living in London by then. 'What are you worried about? You haven't been happy at MBC for ages. You've resigned - move on! Take it. See what happens. You've got nothing to lose.'

So I accepted. We opened for business in Camden Town, just north of Central London, in TV studios which had been a well-known local landmark since the 1980s. We farmed out our network control, that is, our satellite and general technical transmission, to Associated Press who occupied part of the building. Its Chief Executive was Ian Ritchie, a kind and friendly Yorkshireman who had done that job at MBC, so I knew him.

'Let's make this channel successful!' he said. Rafik Khalifa came, and at the end of January 2003 we signed the transmission contract. That was at 1pm and we made the first news broadcast at 6pm. In Dubai they'd been working for months and still hadn't yet gone live.

The second Gulf war was looming: America's stance towards Iraq was becoming increasingly belligerent. Within days we'd got an interview with Saddam Hussein - by Tony Benn, of all people: the grand old man of British socialism, in his seventies at the time. He'd gone to Bagdad with a TV crew, hired an interpreter, and distributed the programme himself. This of course was no ordinary interview, but a discussion between a Ba'athist dictator and a man who had lived and breathed radical politics since childhood. Benn's message was - 'The Americans are going to do you and Iraq a lot of damage. You have to step down from waging war.' Saddam Hussein answered in Arabic.

Ian said - 'We've got this interview. D'you want it?'

'Yes!' I said.

'But Tony Benn's talking English, and the interpreter –'

'It doesn't matter. Saddam Hussein's the one they want to hear.'

We just aired it, without even having time to do a transcript. I got a call afterwards. In Dubai, it seemed, the people at Al Arabiya were reeling with shock. 'How did they *do* that?'

'They hired the right people,' somebody said drily.

I felt glad I'd taken the job. I was still old-MBC at heart but this really worked. It couldn't be better.

By the start of the second week of March, more than 200,000 American troops had already lined up on the Kuwaiti border. I said to Ian

'This is happening. Nobody can stop it. We need somebody there.'

Ian said

'For ten thousand dollars, I can do you a link between studio guests and correspondents in the field.' It was a terrific offer - a bargain rate. Fantastic.

He got me live transmissions from Washington, Jordan and Turkey. Our coverage would pip all the others at the post. I had a cameraman, a freelance, on standby. He promised to fly out as soon as we were ready to send him. I called our correspondent in Turkey; we were all prepared.

I wasn't authorised to release as much money as this and needed to call our finance director. 'Ian needs this signed this off quickly,' I said. 'It's ten thousand dollars. Things are hotting up in Iraq.'

He was an Englishman who worked for both KTV and Khalifa Airlines.

'I'll get back to you,' he said. 'Khalifa needs to check it out.'

'Ron, we're in a hurry. Let him know important it is – if we get it, we'll be really huge. It's about on-the-spot live coverage of the Americans going into Iraq.'

'I'll make that absolutely clear, don't worry. I'll do it as soon as I possibly can but just wait.'

'Okay. But this'll make us.'

I waited, wishing Ron would hurry up and get this out of the way. On Thursday March 14th, 2003, the build-up to the American invasion was in all the papers and every broadcast news bulletin. Then he called.

'Hacene we have an issue.'

'What issue?'

'You have to come to Paris right now. Khalifa's here, he wants to see you.'

'What's this all about?'

'He'll tell you. Don't worry, just come over.'

The Eurostar terminus was at Waterloo in those days. I grabbed my coat, left the building and hailed a taxi. Something must be going on in France. I hadn't seen anything in *Le Monde* this morning. New political scandal, maybe? I had no idea what could be as important as the Iraq invasion, but something clearly was.

Three hours later, I was in a cab from the Gare du Nord to an hotel near the Etoile.

Ron was sitting in the lobby. He waved, stood up, and I joined him.

'It's not good news, I'm afraid. We have a serious cash flow problem. We were expecting money from Algeria. The plane that was bringing it's been stopped and the money's been confiscated.'

The plane? Confiscated? What kind of outfit was I working for? I said

'Hold on. This can't be relevant to KTV. We're on the verge of going to war. You're telling me we can't show the American invasion because we don't have ten thousand dollars to pay for it?'

'We have to cancel, Hacene. We cannot pay. For the moment. For that project.'

'This doesn't make sense. I'm only talking about ten thousand dollars! How much money was on this plane?'

'No idea. Millions.'

What on earth - ? I had to stick to the point. 'We don't need millions! All we need - Look we can't *not* do this, Ron.'

'Sorry, there is to be no further expense. Zero. The cupboard is bare, Hacene.'

'Can I talk to Khalifa?'

'When he gets to London you can. Right now, no. Give it 24 hours and call him at the Dorchester.'

I returned to London almost certain that the ground had shifted beneath my feet, and yet unwilling to believe it. I didn't sleep well and before eight the following morning, March 15th, I called the Dorchester. He was already there. I drove straight to Park Lane, and was told that he would come down to see me.

I sat on a sofa and scanned *The Times*. I caught sight of Rafik Khalifa among the throng that emerged from the lift, answering his mobile phone, pacing up and down behind a gaudy flower arrangement, in shirtsleeves without a tie, talking to somebody. He saw me and made a 'five minutes' signal with his fingers.

When the call ended he trudged across the carpet, dodging waiters with trays of coffee. The urbane Rafi Khalifa who had told me 'money is not an issue' was hard to recognise. He was unsmiling, stubble-chinned, and his shirt looked slept-in. He slumped round-shouldered into an armchair. He seemed about ten years older and exhausted.

'I'm sorry Hacene. Ron told me what you want, but it cannot be done.'

'Please, Mr Khalifa. It's very cheap, this, and it's urgent - the war can begin within hours, and this ten thousand dollars will put KTV on the map - we'll probably never get a chance like this again.'

'No. We cannot put in one penny.'

'But I don't get it. If you don't cover this war you have no KTV! You can sort out your bloody financial problems later.'

'The situation's not in my hands,' he said.

'Well who on earth - whose hands is it in, then?'

He sighed. 'Hacene. I am not in a position to continue with KTV.'

'You're bankrupt?'

'Forget it, Hacene. I really can't discuss it.' He got up. 'You've done a great job, but it's over.'

I bought *Le Monde* and *Le Figaro* at the bookstall and scanned the business pages. And I found something. There wasn't much, but the story evidently went back over a week; I had been too busy with the Gulf crisis and our first broadcasts to notice it. In the Assembly, the leader of the French Green party had accused Khalifa Bank of handling money for the Algerian generals - vast sums which had been intended for the benefit of the Algerian people. Khalifa Bank had been forced to stop trading so, as lease payments fell due and went unpaid, most of the Khalifa Airways fleet was grounded. There was some kind of warrant out for him in France, and had been for a good ten days.

Rafik Khalifa was here, in the Dorchester, on the run.

Ironic, really. I'd always kept up with events, but the one story that affected me personally had been playing out right under my nose and I hadn't seen it.

I went straight back to the office, unobtrusively cleared my desk and left. As I walked out into Hawley Crescent I ran into a friend. Abdurahman Al Rashed was a Saudi who'd become well known as the presenter of a weekly programme on Lebanese TV. He broadcast it from the Associated Press offices here, and when he wasn't doing that, he edited *Al Sharq al Awsat*, the Middle Eastern newspaper published in London. Also, he happened to be friendly with Ali.

I wanted to talk to him, but this wasn't the place or time so I arranged to meet him for lunch later.

This extraordinary day had begun with a surprise and would produce several more, but I didn't know that.

We met at the restaurant shortly after midday. Rahman told me how annoyed he was that Al Sharq's correspondent in Jordan had been put on standby to go to Iraq whenever the invasion took place, but the Iraqis had refused to give her a visa.

I told him that KTV was effectively defunct.

'Listen, I've got a visa,' I said. 'I can go, and I can write the report for you. But on one condition - I want to take a TV cameraman as well. So if you know anybody who's interested in the footage let me know.'

'Terrific. You're on. What kind of fee are we talking about here?'

'We can sort out the money later. I will make sure your page is full of articles and pictures every day. Is that a deal?'

'Yeah,' he said. 'That's a great deal.'

It was a Friday evening and I met my brother for a meal. Action defeats gloom every time, and I was a lot happier. I had a creative new task ahead; I knew I'd be in Iraq, with a cameraman, within days. We were drinking coffee when my phone rang. I fished it out of my pocket.

'It's MBC Dubai.'

'Maybe it's Ali,' said Kader. He meant Sheikh Walid's right-hand man.

It was.

'This is a surprise,' I said. 'Hallo, Ali.'

'Hacene, where are you? Are you going to Bagdad?'

How had he known? I thought I knew. 'Hope so. Right now I'm in London.'

'Can you get a flight to Dubai?'

'Not now - it's after ten, the last one's gone.'

'Well, get the first one in the morning then.'

'What's this about?'

'I can't talk about it. I have a great opportunity for you. Just call me the minute you land. You'll be on the first flight, yeah?'

'Um - ? OK. Yes.'

I switched the phone off. Kader had heard only my end of the conversation and raised his eyebrows. 'Well?'

'It seems I'm flying to Dubai in the morning,' I shrugged. 'He says he's got a great opportunity for me.'

'Sounds good.'

'Fingers crossed.'

'And he already knew I was going to Iraq.'

'Rahman must have told him.'

'My thoughts exactly. So he knows about KTV going down the tubes.'

I drove to Heathrow, caught the first plane in the morning, and there was a car to meet me. I called Ali. 'The hotel's booked for you,' he said. 'Drop your stuff over there and come to my office.'

When I walked into his room at Media City he said

'I want you in Kuwait. I can get you in with the American troops when they invade. Can you do that?'

'I can,' I said. 'But I didn't come here to work. This is a flying visit. I'm here to discuss opportunities with you.'

'Not right now,' he said, 'There's no time for that. No time for discussion, or contracts or anything. I just want you in Kuwait as soon as you can get there. They're refusing visas to everybody. Can you get one?'

'Yes. I know the Kuwaitis. But I left my car at Heathrow –'

He waved that away. 'We can deal with that later. When you get your visa, make your way to Kuwait City as soon as possible. And go downstairs and see Mark.' Mark was Head of News at Al Arabiya. 'He'll give you some money and a Thoraya.' The Thoraya satphone, a useful piece of kit which connected you from arid desert to shining sea just about anywhere, was new on the market at that time. 'He's got a team lined up for you; camera, producer, everything.'

'Look I didn't come here to go to war. I have to call my wife and son.'

'Hacene, do what the hell you like, it's all covered. You know that.' Since Chechnya, there had been a verbal guarantee that MBC would pay double the normal insurance compensation should anything happen.

I rang Tanya at our home in Suffolk, a pretty county of villages and rolling green hills north-east of London. Little Atlas, my five-year old son, barely knew me except as a voice on the phone; this caused me a pang of guilt whenever I saw him.

I also called my brother, who had a spare key to the car at Heathrow, and asked him to pick it up. And I talked to Rahman. He'd get his articles.

The following morning, a Sunday, I got the visa, and by eight that evening I was on a flight to Kuwait City. On Monday morning the American forces issued my accreditation and early in the morning of Tuesday 19th I was talking to the camera as Allied tanks rolled past behind me heading for Basra. This was news, all right – Operation Iraqi Freedom, George W Bush called it. 'Those tanks could be in Bagdad within days,' I reported.

At KTV in Camden, people stared at the screen and said '*What – ?*' They'd seen me in the office last Friday. Three days ago. But they still hadn't been told about the mess Khalifa was in. 'What's Hacene doing in Kuwait? He's supposed to be here.'

We sent several pieces from Kuwait to Dubai in the first 24 hours of the war but the Head of News at Al Arabiya, for reasons best known to himself, did not show them all. This caused a certain flutter in the dovecote. The bureau chief in Kuwait City rang the General Director, who sharply told the man on duty – an Egyptian – to put them out. This Egyptian called me.

'Who employed you?'

'I can't talk now, I'm in a war zone. Please ask Ali or Mark.'

'Why are you bigging up the Americans?'

'I'm not. I'm just reporting what I saw. I'm doing a job here. It's the truth. Bagdad is where they are heading and they'll probably get there.'

So that was it; attempted censorship from quite low down in the hierarchy of control. I stayed for a few weeks. Basra fell, Bagdad was being bombed. I flew out to Dubai, and from there into Bagdad, which was then already under US control.

A month after leaving London, I was back in Dubai again. This time I was presented with a contract to work as an international roving correspondent for Al Arabiya.

'But you will not be based in London.'

'Well, where then? I've got a family to consider.'

'Right now, go back to England. We'll call you when we want you. Don't go into the newsroom. Feelings are running quite high there.'

'Why?'

'You present a challenge to some of the staff.'

This would be a problem. Any editor with a political agenda could –
if unsupervised –simply fail to transmit material that contradicted his
world-view. However, they wanted me to work for them without a fixed
operational base, 'roving', and I was getting paid to do what I enjoyed best,
so – who was I to look a gift horse in the mouth? I'd deal with the internal
politics as and when these issues arose.

I spent a few days in London clearing up my affairs before I went to Suffolk
to join Tanya and Atlas. I was about to leave when I got a call. Crown
Prince Abdullah was to be in Evian for a G8 summit. I went there, covered
the story - it was an important conference - and came back.

Then I went to Suffolk. And waited; and waited.

Chapter 12

Be careful who you work for

I spent the next five weeks at home in England. It was the longest time I had ever spent with my son and my wife. We had a big house with swimming pool, and beautiful weather. Every morning it was warm enough to jump in the pool. I taught Atlas to swim, and I got to know him. I played football with him and took him to the cinema.

The phone did not ring. I didn't care. After four weeks,I called to see if my salary had been paid, and it had; and life was great. A fifth week went by, and a sixth had just started. I was beginning to think that this was rather odd, but who was I to complain?

We were now well into June. At last a Lebanese lady called from Al Arabiya's Human Resources department.

'Hacene, I am calling to invite you to Dubai.'

'OK.'

'I have a London number for you to call. Ask for Aisha there and she'll arrange your flight tickets and the hotel.'

'How long d'you want me to stay?'

'She'll book you two weeks at the Hilton.'

So I flew there and reported to the newsroom. 'That's fine, Hacene. We know you're around. Just wait and we'll call you – drop by in the mornings whenever you feel like it.'

I spent my afternoons by the Hilton pool or in the shopping mall or the souk, my evenings at the cinema or eating alone and watching TV, and my mornings reading the papers in the newsroom.

Every morning I had a sofa, a coffee table and a pile of papers and magazines all to myself. The Egyptian Head of News and the producers, many of whom I knew from London, didn't say a word. They walked past without apparently noticing that I was there.

I was getting a salary, a room with a view and full board, and £50 a day for my expenses, but I was just kicking my heels. One day I was sitting at a computer when Ali found me.

'Hey, Hacene! What are you up to?'

'Nothing. There's nothing for me.'

'How long have you been here?'

'Nearly two weeks.'

'You mean you haven't had anything in that time? Have you been going to the morning meeting?'

'I'm not invited to that.'

'Go up to my office. I'll be with you in two minutes.'

We sat down and talked.

'I'm beginning to feel like the Invisible Man,' I said. I told him about my five weeks of gardening leave. 'And then I got a call from HR, not the newsroom, and I was asked to come all this way. And - still nothing. I'm here every day but nobody talks to me. I think hell, was it something I said?'

I was only half joking. I felt aggrieved, and especially since I missed Tanya and Atlas. Ali made it clear that this hadn't been supposed to happen. I was too diplomatic to explain that when people promised him that they'd do something, they'd often go ahead and do its opposite. He had a big job and omissions could slip past him.

He said 'OK, forget all that. I've got a job for you. But it's very hush-hush. We're going to be doing a big interview soon. I want a seven minute piece about Al-Sahhaf, his life and times, from stock. You'll find it all in the library.'

'Sure.' Mohammed Al Sahhaf was Saddam Hussein's spokesman, famous for boasting about how Iraq could never be conquered and Saddam Hussein was the great leader, father of the nation, guiding beacon of civilisation and so on, and so on.

'I want it for tomorrow. Don't tell anybody what you're doing. I'll tell the library to keep quiet.' I spent the rest of that day finding everything we'd got about Al-Sahhaf, drafting a running order and cutting key clips together.

I booked a short time in a studio in the early evening, and briefly ran through an intro in front of a blown-up picture of the man. I was doing this when the hostile Egyptian walked in.

'What are you doing?'

'Working. If you don't want me to, other people do.'

'What is this?'

'I don't have to tell you; I have to finish it.'

Around eleven o'clock on the Wednesday night I put the tape on Ali's desk and left. The next morning, they started with my report and went on to the interview. To get an exclusive with a person like that was a big scoop. I went to see Ali.

'Great stuff. Gave the interview more of a build-up. More substance. Thanks, Hacene.'

'Glad you liked it. But I'm going back to London. Having me hanging about here is costing you a lot of money. I am doing nothing. I'm not committed here and I'm at a loose end in England. So when the guys have made up their minds to use me, just get them to make a phone call.'

I went home for another two or three weeks on full pay. I was getting the same passive-aggressive treatment that had so annoyed me in my last years at MBC. They didn't say yes, they didn't say no, and being in limbo is tough.

Finally the Human Resources lady called to invite me for another fortnight in Dubai.

'Why? Is there any work for me this time? Because last time, you know, there really wasn't.'

'No, this time it's serious. They want you back for two weeks so that you can find accommodation for you and your family.'

'I'm not staying there.'

'The decision is made. You have to come.'

It was pointless to argue with her, because she was just an employee like me. I told her I'd come, but I'd already decided that this was my breaking point.

'You know why they are doing this,' I said to Tanya. 'They know I don't want to live there. They're forcing me to resign.'

'Why would they do that?'

'Because I won't be their problem any more. I'm the awkward squad. I don't like being pushed around and I keep doing good stuff but sometimes it's not what they want to hear.'

'Hacene, I've been thinking. How bad can Dubai be? Why are we always so negative about it?'

'It's a dump to live in. It's so bloody hot. You'd die there if it wasn't for air conditioning. Every time I go there I think, what am I doing to the planet? It's artificial. It's superficial. It's a bubble full of meaningless –'

'OK, I know. But everywhere's got disadvantages. There are whole months here when Atlas can't play outside because it's so cold. Let's just go and see.'

'What, you mean come with me for the two weeks and –'

'No. You've signed a contract with them. Tell them we'll live there and see how it goes. There are schools – We won't have to burn our boats here. We can afford the mortgage on top of everything else, or maybe rent it out - what have we got to lose?'

I flew out, rented an unfurnished flat and chose furniture which MBC Group paid for. At home, Tanya put a lot of things into store and prepared to leave at the end of Atlas's first school year.

I worked from the Al Arabiya newsroom in Dubai. Most of the time I was just writing news reports and doing pieces to camera in the newsroom for Panorama, a programme that went out at 8pm London time. Six days a week, I went to the studios at 1pm for a meeting with the news editor and presenter, and we decided on the main report of the day. Fallujah, the Iraqi city, was the focus of a lot of interest because some American contractors had been murdered by a mob and the Americans were determined to subdue the place and gain control.

It was regular work with very few foreign assignments, and every reason for Tanya and Atlas to be happy. When they finally joined me, Tanya didn't like the accommodation I'd rented, so I cancelled that agreement and took instead a lovely villa with a pool. I had a superb car and we enrolled Atlas in one of the best schools in Dubai. We had very little to complain about.

Foreign assignments were rare. Once I had to go and report on the talks between North and South Sudan at Lake Naivasha. And a few months later when a huge truck bomb killed the British Consul-General in Istanbul, they sent me there.

After less than a year in Dubai, Tanya and I were not getting on. We were both bored. Atlas was happy, but she and I had run out of entertainment; we seemed to have explored all the malls, restaurants and leisure facilities of Dubai and its novelty value had worn off. It didn't have an accessible cultural hinterland, and Tanya was simply homesick. I liked being with the family, but my job didn't seem to be leading anywhere and that made me grumpy. If anything the job felt like a step backwards.

I went to see Ali, explained and asked to return to Europe. He offered me Paris. I accepted at once. I'd be only two hours by air from Setif, my home town.

'But you'll be working for MBC, not Al Arabiya.'

'Fine. I don't mind which it is.'

'OK. Well, make your way there as soon as you can.'

I was happy. Atlas would grow up speaking French, English and Arabic. We decided that keeping our beautiful English home made no sense. We would be living in Paris and we couldn't justify leaving the place empty for five years.

We sold some stuff, packed some stuff, Tanya went to Suffolk with Atlas to sell the house and arrange the move, and I settled in an apartment in Paris and started work. We bought a house in Normandy, and filled it with our antiques. The house in Suffolk was sold, and Atlas had been accepted at a bilingual International School in Versailles.

And then, one night, Tanya rang.

'Hacene. Atlas doesn't want to live in France.'

But this wasn't altogether about Atlas. Tanya wanted to stay in Suffolk as well; effectively to live separately. And then, having sold the lovely Georgian place we'd had, she bought instead a boring little house outside a small town. It was the beginning of the end of our marriage anyway.

I spent five years in France working for MBC and sometimes for Al Arabiya, seeing less and less of my son as he grew. I used to hire a car and drive all the way to Suffolk from London, or sometimes take my own car all the way to Calais, then on the ferry to Dover, and then on up to their new house (a round trip of about 1,000 kilometers there and back). I had a small but beautiful rented flat in Paris; but they did not want to come there. I kept the relationship with Atlas going. But - Tanya and I remain good friends, although we divorced when our son was eight. One day, I got a document in the post, and signed it, and sent it back; and that was that.

Of course, it wasn't entirely the job's fault. But if you are a foreign correspondent (or anyone who often has to travel on business, some of it dangerous, all of it at unpredictable times) there has to be a level of understanding on both sides. For instance, somebody who has just come back after a month under fire in a war zone doesn't want to discover that he and the family have to fly out the following day for a holiday in the Caribbean. He wants to lie down.

Equally, it would be nice if your partner's employer understood that no-one with children can be expected to work 24/7, 365 days a year.

People of both sexes suffer from the difficulties of this job. Most of us are men, and I've lost count of the number who have told me that they blame the job for their divorce. There are distinguished female war reporters:

Christiane Amanpour, Kate Adie, Marie Colvin (who was killed in Beirut), Zeina Awad are examples who don't have children.

If you do, the key to a successful marriage may well be shared understanding of the work. Frances Harrison worked for the BBC on dangerous assignments for more than a decade, including almost her entire pregnancy and her son's early childhood. Her Iranian husband is also a BBC TV reporter. Alex Crawford of Sky News has four children and a husband at home and was in Gaddafi's compound when it fell to the opposition. Her interviews, on camera, with a bunch of adrenalin-fuelled rebels firing off celebratory AK-47s were a scoop. How does she do it? Firstly, she had been a TV news journalist for twenty years before she became a foreign correspondent. Secondly, her partner too is a journalist so he understands what her job means. When he retired to look after the children, they discussed together what would be a new career for her, how her work in war zones might affect the balance of power in the relationship, and how their domestic lives would be organised.

The Harrison and Crawford households no doubt have problems as every couple does, but they are both fully committed to the situation. If you are a young female journalist in the Arab world with ambitions to become a foreign correspondent, such commitment from a husband may be hard to find. It can challenge a person who's conditioned to dominate a marriage.

There's a third reason why the job can be made to work for Frances Harrison, Alex Crawford and others like them. Sky News and the BBC are western employers. They don't offer patronage, but rock-solid contracts. They're not perfect, but contracts of employment, by law in the west, cover regular holidays, adequate notice, maternity leave, holiday pay, training programmes, expensive insurance, reasonable hours, grievance procedures and sometimes crèches. If you have worked as a foreign correspondent for five or six years you are first in line for a job as presenter.

Arab channels are sloppy about these things because they are fundamentally paternalistic. If they employ you, they feel they've bought you. They take responsibility for you, and they're extremely generous, but they also call the shots without fear of being challenged. They assume that your marriage and children are vastly less important than your job. (In the west, this is not the case.) They dislike challenge.

And they may dispose of you on a whim, because they fail to see that by getting experience a worker becomes an asset - an enhanced human resource who should be used to train the next generation.

I would have made more of an effort, I think, to stay in Dubai and make it work if I'd had my own current affairs programme. As it was, someone else was always in control of my schedule. And given that my schedule was limitless, this state of not knowing, not having a defined outcome or a set aim, was intensely stressful.

I learned, in that five years in Paris, that work shouldn't take over your life. I learned to relax, and I refuse to do a 24 hour working day.

In Afghanistan once, reporting for Al Arabiya, I finished work at about 11.45 one night. The curfew started at midnight, so the Turkish company that had organised the news-feed for me gave me a lift to my hotel. I got in just before lockdown.

I was fast asleep when the phone rang. I squinted at the display. 01.50. It was the news editor, from Dubai.

'Hacene? We want you on camera.'

'I just finished live to you two hours ago. There's a curfew, you know that. I can't leave the hotel and the camera can't come here. Nobody moves.'

'Damn. You want to do it over the phone?'

'Do what? I've been asleep. What've I got to say? D'you think I've been interviewing the Taliban at two o'clock in the morning?'

'Well -'

'I've been *asleep*.'

'So shall I just say we spoke and nothing has changed?'

'Say what you like. If you wake me up to work in the middle of the night do I get extra money?'

After that I used to switch the phone off at night, which didn't go down well at all.

'Why's your phone been off? That's unacceptable! This is 24 hour news!'

'I don't work a 24-hour day. You need to employ more people. Or pay extra.'

'You're so intransigent. This is just unprofessional.'

'If you think it's professional to expect people to work for nothing you should think again. Or pay me overtime. Or find a shift worker.'

It really was insane to be asked, for no particular reason, to work at two o'clock in the morning - which was one in the morning in Dubai, where most people would be tucked up in bed anyway.

However in Paris, working for MBC rather than Al Arabiya, I did begin enjoying my work again. MBC Paris were happy to make programmes about everyday life. I had to film sick people sometimes, which was distressing, but not as frustrating as the emotional barrage of a war zone. I interviewed doctors, attended conferences on the environment, did a piece about the Pasteur Institute and covered all sorts of domestic issues, not just in France but in Belgium, the Netherlands and Switzerland.

We rented premises from a Parisian production company who provided us with everything; maybe that added too much to our costs. When MBC began cutting its European budget in 2008/9 Paris was closed down and

I was offered a job back in London. Battersea was shut, but they had now had studios on the South Bank near Lambeth Bridge, just upstream of the Houses of Parliament. I moved back in 2010 and was happy to see more of my son. Otherwise, I was back with that old uncertain feeling...

In 2010 MBC in London still suffered from the management failures that had bedevilled it a decade before: ignorance and indecision caused by putting the wrong people in the job. It wasn't that they were stupid. It's just that they didn't understand television and had got jobs with big salaries because criteria for selection barely existed. This is the Arab way - to look after your friends first.

And competition for ratings was allowed to supersede competence. In Arab TV generally, pretty women (as opposed to skilled female TV journalists) are hired to present the news because they attract a big audience. Sooner or late it becomes clear that they're out of their depth, and they're replaced by a new pretty face rather than a more knowledgeable female journalist. Nobody wins. Nobody with a long-term view would let it happen.

I thought again of MBC in the late 90s, when most of the BBC people had gone and this cultural problem soon became apparent. The new guys never did understand that you get what you pay for. In the early 90s, we'd had two full-time cameramen and two sound engineers. But when the Arab newcomers came, and saw that a three-man crew meant travel, accommodation and per diem costs x 3, they decided to make cost savings. From then on, we used different cameramen and I never knew who I'd be working with.

Sandy Gall knew that for optimum use of time and consistent quality, you and your cameraman think as one. You don't have to issue ideas or suggestions or instructions to one another; you have learned to work in unison, and when it comes to cutting the piece, you know what you want the shots to say. Commitment is key. Alex Crawford in Gaddafi's compound had a cameraman who, as viewers could tell, was badly jostled at one point by a hostile crowd. The pictures were disturbed but didn't stop coming; he kept shooting. He stuck with the situation. He worked with the same determination she did.

But for me it was 'You go, and we'll hire you a cameraman and an editor.' I never knew whether I'd get somebody creative and quick on the uptake, or a guy who just stood there waiting for direction, or someone who'd pull out at the last minute.

Once or twice by pure fluke they found me somebody outstanding. When I went to Chechnya to cover its second war, in 1999, I had Yuri, an old man from Moscow who brought along his son as assistant. I noticed he had a beautiful camera.

We had to drive through Dagestan en route. All I'd said to Yuri was 'we're looking for human-interest today.' We saw a trainload of refugees that had stopped in the middle of nowhere. The train had windows, but otherwise it could have been an image from World War II of the cattle-trucks into which Jews and gypsies were crammed en route for death in Treblinka or Auschwitz.

The railway gauge in Russia is wide, and where there is no platform, the carriages loom high above the ground. 'Stop here,' Yuri said. He had seen an old man alone in a white wilderness, making his way to say goodbye his family on that train. And he knew exactly how to shoot it. The lined anxious face, the ponderous trudge in deep snow, the view from below of the intimidatingly high carriage and the passengers in distress, told the story without words. When the piece was transmitted Edwin Hart called me. 'Who's working with you?' I told him about Yuri. 'He's worked in cinema. He's the one who shot the Siberian bears.'

'Ah,' he said. 'No wonder. Brilliant stuff. Congratulations.' I was delighted, knowing that I had never been Edwin's favourite person; and Yuri was pleased when I told him. He had said to me

'Hacene I was clothed entirely in white, and covered in snow, but that bear could have killed me instantly. He could not see me but I was literally a few metres away.'

The close-ups of the bears, and the angles he got – all the newsmen had watched the BBC series about Russian wildlife, *Realms of the Russian Bear,* and the clip of the bears in Siberia got played over and over. That kind of cinematography shouldn't be compromised and if a correspondent wants to take a good cameraman or editor with him, it's not because he's doing a mate a favour – he's trying to help make the channel he works for more respected than any other. Just one story can make a difference. Yuri got me some great stuff.

The quality of the cinematography, the ability to make an image worth a thousand words, is ignored on Arab TV channels. There's more to showing an event than just pointing a camera. When I see the best of European documentary I can tell that they have invested money in aiming for perfection. The name of the game is not 'a story' but 'a well-told story'. It's an attitude Arab TV would do well to learn. After all, it isn't as if we don't have enough money or the best technology.

Good production management means money is not wasted. In the mid-nineties I went to Africa to report on the conflict between North and South Sudan. In the early days our management would have been persuaded to send two correspondents, one to each side, as in Yemen. Not any more; I was supposed to report from the North, then from the South. And this wasn't easy because actually there were four key players, not just two.

To understand this story you need a simplified mental image of three countries on the map. Sudan (which at the time was one big unit) is enormous. Its eastern border skirts both the Red Sea and a much smaller country, Eritrea. Eritrea also has a long Red Sea coastline. South-east of Sudan, and south of Eritrea, is Ethiopia, which is big but landlocked.

Eritrea had become so annoyed by radical Islamists pouring in from Sudan that it had broken off diplomatic relations with Khartoum in 1994 and closed the border.

In Sudan, the South wanted to secede from the more Islamic North. Many South Sudanese rebels took advantage of the border dispute by making their way across Ethiopia and up to Eritrea across its other border. Eritrea became a base from which they could attack the North in a pincer movement, allied to guerrilla attacks from South Sudan itself.

So for North Sudan, Eritrea was hostile and Ethiopia was far from friendly, and the South Sudanese had to be fought on two fronts. My brief was to report first from the point of view of the North, then from the South.

From Khartoum we first went to south-east to Kassala, where the northern forces were confronting the South-Sudanese along the Eritrean border. And then, even further south to a place called Al Damazin, nearer to the border with Ethiopia. The Roseires Dam there was at the time the main source of hydro-electric power for the whole country, and the South Sudanese were trying get control of it, or sabotage it. It was a mighty construction: a kilometer of concrete about seventy meters high with massive long earthworks on either side. We filmed fighting there.

I was now supposed to cover the South-Sudanese forces. To get their angle on it I had to go around their front line and towards them via Ethiopia. So the cameraman and I, and our equipment, were driven back to Khartoum. We flew from there to Addis Ababa. There I was able to get an appointment with the Prime Minister of Ethiopia to find out what he thought of the North/South/Eritrea conflict, and after the interview I asked him whether he could facilitate my access to the South Sudanese by letting us cross his country as far as the border where the fighting was.

He agreed, so we then had to drive, and it was a long way. What I saw as we drove west astonished me. My expectations were quite different, for the TV images from Ethiopia's devastating famine in the eighties were still with me. I remembered malnourished children on a dusty plain. There was no dusty plain where we went, and the children looked perfectly well. We took a four-wheel drive over bumpy tracks up mountainsides and through jungles where monkeys swung through the trees, colourful birds flashed by, and a huge feline slipped away as we turned a bend in the road 'Was that a leopard?' I could hardly believe what I'd seen. A mile further on, round thatched mud huts clustered in a clearing where chickens pecked the ground, and wizened black gentlemen sat smoking pipes.

We arrived at Kurmuk, a South-Sudanese town of the plain, close to the Ethiopian border. The people of Kurmuk did not seem pleased to see any of us. Our party consisted of a driver from Addis Ababa, our producer from Addis who spoke Arabic and Ethiopian, me, and an English cameraman. I don't know what exactly they objected to, but maybe they'd seen too many media, passing through without spending money. Anyway we crossed a river to get to the rebel troops. I'd expected an army but this was a rabble; they were gathered around a fire, smoking, idling and talking. We relaxed under mango trees and they sacrificed a goat for us. Admittedly none of these guys gave us a coherent interview, but we got our shots of their camp, a great meal and an experience to remember. It was a beautiful country. What next?

We were supposed to give every side of this conflict so we had to get into Eritrea somehow. The only way was to go to Asmara, the capital. Since Eritrea had fallen out with both neighbours, Ethiopia as well as Sudan, there were no direct flights. We would have to fly from Khartoum to London and directly from there to Asmara. The simplest way from Kurmuk to Khartoum was by road; but we couldn't do that since we would have to cross the war zone between North and South. Instead we had to drive all the way back to Addis Ababa; then fly to London; then get flights back to Asmara. It took days and cost far too much.

In TV, planning for economy works in peacetime, if, for instance, you're covering an American Presidential election. You have a set time, and a predictable schedule. In a war zone the cheapest way – the way we were doing it in Sudan – is not remotely fast enough and always ends up costing more. Anybody who does a cost-benefit analysis of an operation like this quickly realises that a false economy such as sending the same two guys to four or five inaccessible places in succession will end up costing a fortune. The cameraman and I were crawling from point to point for ten or fourteen days and by the time we'd done so the story was dying. An efficiently-run network would have saved money, and received immediate and contemporary reports from all sides, by using three crews at once in different places. They'd have been there and back in three days with fresh, immediate news.

Would MBC ask for advice on logistics and costings from a mere correspondent? No, because they don't value TV experience.

Chapter 13

Arab Spring

Late in December of 2010, in a town in Tunisia called Sidi Bouzid, a street vendor called Mohamed Bouazizi had borrowed money to stock his cart with vegetables. He piled them high, trundled the cart to market first thing in the morning, and started selling. A couple of hours later the police arrived. They had harassed him before. This time they threatened to arrest him. They said he needed a permit (he didn't). They demanded bribes and when he refused to pay, they beat him up.

Bouazizi had put up with this kind of thing for years. And for years, in spite of it, he had somehow earned enough to feed his family. But today, under special pressure because he was indebted, he had had enough. He asked to see the Governor. He was turned away. He stood in the town square and shouted about corruption and the cruelty of treating an honest man like this. He doused himself with petrol, and set himself alight.

I read about Bouazizi's self-immolation and the thousands of angry sympathisers who poured onto the streets when he died. Fury flashed around the country and broke out in Tunis. A poor street trader had set the whole country alight. I quickly checked flight availability. There was nothing direct from London, but if I got the Eurostar to Paris I'd be in time to catch the last flight of the night out of Orly to Tunis. I told my editor in Dubai that this was worth covering, and I should get there fast.

'So is that OK? I'll book it now.'

'Hold on - hold on. We'll get back to you.'

I had seen something big starting in Tunisia, a revolution on the streets. But by the time they decided to say no to me, all flights out of Paris had been grounded anyway.

Eventually – when other networks were already there, and reporting back – they sent a correspondent from Algeria. Then there was Egypt, and Algeria itself – an eruption of protest that consumed the Maghreb and was called the Arab Spring. But somebody else was sent to report on all of it.

Then, many weeks after the start of the Arab Spring, Libya. A popular uprising so vehement that everyone thought it would end Gaddafi's régime.

'Hacene, we want you to go.'

'Thanks, but you do need continuity.' If a reporter is the first to report on a story, his research usually enriches any similar stories that he covers subsequently. He's heard about the issues, and he can spot what's different and what's alike between associated places and people. I wriggled on the hook. 'You've got people who've been following it so far and - you know, the Arab Spring is really all one story. Besides it will be hard for me to get in at all.'

'You're the best person to go.'

Why this flattery all of a sudden? 'I really would rather not.'

'Please – we want you to go. Really. You must go, Hacene.'

In other words, were I to refuse, there could be consequences that I might not like. So in March 2011, I gave in to the pressure.

Chapter 14

Fear

I was normally keen to go into the field, to war zones, but when it came to Libya - I was not. I told myself that I'd seen colleagues from other channels go there and come home unscathed, so I had nothing to worry about. And I learned the backstory, or at least some of the thinking that had brought pressure to bear on me. A freelance reporter, domiciled in Libya, who had often worked for MBC over the years, had come under suspicion as having been a tool of Gaddafi. This had forced him to flee to Cairo with his family. Then the Libyan régime, on instructions from Saif al-Islam Gaddafi the dictator's son, had organised a week-long press visit from Dubai to Tripoli and back, and MBC had sent two correspondents on the plane. I don't know what went wrong – whether MBC didn't like the footage or what; I was not fully engaged with events in Libya at the time. I'd heard about it but for me, reporting from Libya was somebody else's problem.

Only after that did the people in Dubai start saying 'This is your thing Hacene, you should be there, this is your job' and after that... '*GO.*'

Since I wasn't embedded with the régime I had to organise my own way of getting in. By then Libya was divided, the western coastal cities, including Tripoli, being under Gaddafi's control, and the eastern ones - specifically Benghazi, the second biggest city - in rebel hands. In Dubai they told me I could either fly into Tunisia, and cross the border into Gaddafi's territory, or enter from Egypt via El Alamein and reach Benghazi by road – in which case I would be with the opposition.

I rang around journalists I knew who'd been there before me. 'Go in with the opposition,' they said. I'd intended to anyway, but I was glad to have my feeling confirmed. One of them gave me the address of the media accreditation centre in Benghazi.

'Amazing place, was some bureaucrat's office until January.'

'Where do people stay?'

'The Tibesti but you need to get in early. You'll never get a reservation - it's pot luck.'

I wanted to take a team from London. 'Too expensive', Dubai said. 'We've got people in Cairo.' It was a short assignment, seven to ten days, so I flew to Cairo and met an Egyptian producer and cameraman. We would take a taxi to the rebel-controlled Libyan border, and then walk across. It was a well-trodden media path and there would be taxis waiting on the Libyan side.

The cameraman and I checked all MBC's equipment including the camera and the Bgan. This is a laptop-sized terminal that will feed your audio and video live, rapidly and faultlessly, from pretty well anywhere with a clear sky, to anywhere else on earth, by Inmarsat. I'd be sending direct to Dubai.

I asked the cameraman if he'd filmed across the border before, and he had. He'd worked for a week in rebel-held territory for Al Arabiya. Majdi, the producer, had worked for Al Arabiya before as well, and he knew the road into Libya and had some useful contacts. I was relieved. I'd be working with guys who were competent, experienced and helpful. We all said goodnight and arranged to meet in the lobby of my hotel at 6am.

At six am the taxi arrived. The producer had shown up, but there was no sign of the cameraman. At 6.10 I called his house. His wife answered. 'He's not going.'

Damn. 'He's not ill, is he?'

'No. But he's not going. He's made the decision.'

MBC's policy, which I respect them for, is never to make anybody go to a war zone if they don't want to. But I had to call Dubai. They promised to get back to me. Less than an hour later they did.

'Don't worry. We've found you a replacement. Go to Alexandria and you'll find him there.'

At mid-morning Majdi and I were in Alexandria but the guy didn't show up. There was nobody. We waited; still nobody came, and we didn't have a contact number. We had lunch. I thought: *I want to go back to Cairo and get a flight to London.* I called MBC in Cairo. 'Where is this cameraman?'

'We'll be in touch.'

We were running out of time. Even if the guy turned up now, we would arrive six or seven hours later than we'd expected.

It was early afternoon. I was beginning to wonder whether the alleged cameraman existed at all. I was sitting in the heat in a coffee shop, calling the bureau in Cairo, the bureau in Dubai... 'What's going on?' Nobody could give me a sensible answer.

We offloaded all the kit and I sent the taxi back. We sat in the café surrounded by equipment. Finally they called.

'Book yourselves into a hotel and you'll have your cameraman in the morning.'

The following morning, at last, a guy arrived. 'I'm the cameraman.'

'Have you worked for MBC before?'

'Not MBC, no.'

'But you do know how to film news in the field?'

'Yeah, yeah.'

'Can you edit?

'I can't edit,' he said, 'but I can film.'

'Can you work the Bgan?'

'The....?' He had never seen a Bgan before. I wasn't overwhelmed with confidence in this guy. Maybe it was the way he stared at the equipment instead of actually handling it. I had heard that the only tricky bit, with the Bgan, was getting the GPS connection in the first place, but I had never done it. When I checked in with Dubai they told me not to worry.

'When you're ready to use it, just call - we've got techies who can talk him through it. Just get into Libya and it'll be fine.'

They had no idea. Nip along to Alexandria, breeze through the border into a shooting war, dodge the hail of bullets and call the office for instructions - They were making this sound like a walk in the park. I was getting bad feelings.

'OK,' I said to the two Egyptians. 'Let's go.'

We found a taxi that would drive us from Alexandria all the way to the border. Around El Alamein we saw big signs, the colour of dried blood, warning of landmines over mile after mile of flat desert. Millions of mines were laid by the British and the Nazis during World War II and despite a long-term clearance operation there are still so many that the land is inaccessible. The oil and gas deposits under that sand could boost the Egyptian economy considerably, but clearance will take years yet.

The sky darkened and big drops of rain splashed down. As Sallum, the border village near the coast, lay ahead and we could see a long queue of cars.

Officials on the Egyptian side didn't care who crossed westwards into Libya; even Egyptians could go, as long as they could show media passes, and we all got through easily. Within a few metres, there stood the rebels. They issued us with forms to fill in, checked them and gave us copies, and we were free to move. It was early afternoon.

The taxi had been arranged for us. 'Benghazi?' We scuttled across to the car and piled in, now lashed by rain. There were a lot of taxis and scores of other journalists and NGO people.

Our route zig-zagged up two or three thousand feet of green, forested hillside. Coming down on the other side of the road, entire families in big cars raced by in the wet. Well-off Libyans were leaving home while they still could, to rent a place in Cairo for the duration.

The rain was torrential, so we decided not to proceed after dark for fear of skidding and tipping the car into a ravine. We stopped and had dinner at a wayside hotel in a small town. A crowd started shouting outside. The waiter said they were excited because of a rumour that Aisha Gaddafi, the dictator's daughter, had been killed. I had no way of confirming whether she had or not, but I asked the cameraman to take a few shots of the demo anyway.

'OK,' he said, 'but I don't have a cover for the camera and it might get wet.'

'Get an umbrella or something, I'll hold it for you.' He turned on the camera and pointed it at the crowds, who seemed elated despite jumping about in teeming rain. I was distracted by getting wet, people bellowing all around, and the fact that I really wasn't sure what was going on. All I wanted was a shower and bed.

We set off early the following day, and drove down to the plain and Benghazi. The streets were mostly empty and the shops shut. The poor, who had no choice but to stay, were involved of necessity. You saw boys, not always in uniform, but always with Kalashnikovs, checking cars and stopping people all over the city.

We found the hotel where the media were staying. We were two or three days later than I'd expected and we couldn't get in.

'Sorry sir, we're full up,' said the manager.

'Not even one room?'

'Not a single one sir.'

'There must be somewhere,' I said. I wanted to let the taxi go, and we'd got bags and equipment to offload. I didn't relish the prospect of traipsing from one reception desk to the next.

'You see that place across the street behind the restaurant? Go down there and you might find a room for the three of you.' We jumped back into the cab. They had two rooms left so Majdi and the cameraman took one and I took the other. Then we went back to the Tibesti to be issued with accreditation. I slung mine round my neck as usual, and tucked it under my shirt. It was just a piece of card, the size of a business card, with my name and 'MBC' on it: not even a photograph, or any sort of official-looking stamp. I hoped it would work.

I made phone calls and went down to the lobby. I saw other journalists, and the hotel guys knew MBC. I'd worked in Libya before, and I found a local fixer I knew. He said – 'Come through here.' He led me to the street entrance near the road and stood inside.

'You see that hotel down by the mosque?' I saw a nondescript multi-storey hotel. 'Abdul Jalil is staying there.' Abdul Jalil was the leader of the Interim Council, which had recently been set up to co-ordinate the opposition. 'All his guys are with him. And I believe an American crew turned up to talk to him this morning.'

'I want an interview,' I said. 'Who do I talk to?'

'This guy.' He wrote a number on a piece of paper and handed it to me. 'Mourad, he's your man. Give him a call.'

I did, and the guy said

'Sure. If you come over now you can grab five minutes – he's giving some interviews.'

We hurried across the road, the producer carrying the tripod, and found the security office. They told us to go in. I felt fired up with enthusiasm. At last we were working, and a scoop like this would set us up for the whole trip.

'Are you ready to go?' I asked the cameraman. 'You've got the sound worked out OK?'

'Yeah,' he said. 'All fine.'

We went inside. I introduced us while they set up the camera and tripod, no lights. Abdul Jalil offered us dates and drinks and we started the interview. I kept it short, asked two or three pointed questions, and got good answers. We wrapped up and left. I called MBC from the lobby of our hotel, told them what we'd got and that I was about to send it over. I took the tape, and Majdi and I walked back to the Tibesti. MBC's transmission was being handled by a production company that had booked a floor there, to service the networks. I found them waiting for us on the roof, having had the booking through from Dubai. Their guy, Nassim, took the tape and I quickly put my name on various bits of paperwork.

'Hacene? There's something wrong.' I turned back to Nassim. I looked at the screen.

'I don't believe it.'

Abdul Jalil was hopelessly out of focus. The angle was off. And worst of all - the sound was inaudible.

'Who is your cameraman?' Nassim asked.

I was too angry to answer. 'Get him over here,' I said to Majdi. 'Hey - Did he tell you he wasn't a pro?'

'No! We talked about football.'

I got on the phone to MBC in Dubai. The person who'd hired this idiot wasn't there - or more likely didn't dare to talk to me. 'Feed it over anyway,' was the message. 'We'll see what we can salvage.' I was about to answer when the guy walked in, looking scared. I cut the call and said to him

'You say you're a cameraman. You're not. You're a liar. You've never used a camera like ours in your life, have you?'

'I'm really sorry.' He was wringing his hands.

'You're *sorry*? Do you know what a mess you've made? How the hell did you get this job? What did you tell them in Dubai?'

'I told them, I make wedding videos, I use a Panasonic. I said I might not know the camera. They said I'd be fine. They told me not to say anything.'

'You're a fool. Pack your stuff and make your own way back to Egypt.'

He started to cry. 'But I haven't got the money to –'

'That's your problem. You can crawl there for all I care. Get out of my sight! I'm not wasting any more MBC money on you. I never want to set eyes on you again.' I was furious. I kept thinking *Why didn't I look at the stuff he shot last night*? I'd been too tired. Right now, the production company people were shaking their heads and laughing at this man. 'Why did you take the risk? This is not a joke. If you didn't know how to do it you should've said so.'

I called Dubai again. 'I'm leaving,' I said. 'I'm going back to Cairo. You're sending me rubbish. If this is the best you can do, you can forget it.'

'No you're there, listen, get a local cameraman, we'll pay, somebody you trust –'

'Why should I bloody well do your job?'

'Calm down. There must be somebody. It's difficult hiring people when you're a long way away, you don't know, and everybody's been booked –'

'Booking's your job. If you'd sent a team from London in the first place I wouldn't be here three days after everybody else has scooped the news. It's your incompetence that's landed me in this pile of dung and now you can't even hire a cameraman.'

'Hacene please – at least ask the production people. They might know somebody. Give it a go, you're there now.'

'I'll ask. But if they don't know anybody I'm going back to London and you can find somebody else to pick up your mess.'

I talked to the production company. 'There's a young chap, Libyan, used to work for Libyan TV. His stuff's fine. He's done some freelance work in Benghazi. We can call him,' Nassim said.

'Okay. Please do.'

The maker of wedding videos was still cowering in a corner, in tears, not wanting to leave.

'I am really sorry. If there is anything I can do to help –'

'What can you do for me? Nothing. Go *away*.'

I couldn't shift him so I ignored him from then on.

A young man turned up. 'You're Hacene? Nassim tells me you need a cameraman. My name's Mohamed Alsouhidi.'

'OK. Do you understand news filming?'

'Yes.'

'I ask you because we travel light. We don't have time to play our stuff back on site. We don't carry a monitor. We shoot and go, and we don't get a second chance. Nassim, show Mohamed the disaster this morning, would you?' Nassim put the tape on and we watched for about forty excruciating seconds. 'You see? This isn't a training program. It's important. I have to have somebody who gets it right first time.'

'OK,' said Mohamed. 'Let's go out, I'll film whatever you want, and you watch it. I'll work for you if you are happy with the results.'

We'd heard about a training camp where young people, supporters of the opposition, learned how to use arms. I didn't know whether they were child soldiers being indoctrinated, or what. So we drove out to the place – an abandoned army base well stocked with old Russian armaments. The boys were sixteen to eighteen years old, full of bravado and nervous as hell underneath. They were a lot like the ones I'd seen toting Kalashnikovs in the streets.

The trainers were ex-Army, and I found one who would give me an interview.

'How much training do you give these kids?' I asked.

'Three weeks.'

'What do you teach them?'

'Weapons training, handling of anti-tank weapons, general discipline.'

'So when they leave where do they go?'

'The front line, in most cases.'

I thought of Atlas, my own son. He would be sixteen next month. His life, I thanked God, was a world away from this.

The footage was good, and MBC broadcast the report. Then Mohamed said

'I think I may know somebody who could ask Abdul Jalil to do the interview again.'

'Thanks – but I don't know... I'd be really embarrassed,' I said.

'We can say there's been a technical hitch.'

'Well... OK then. There's no harm in asking.'

So Abdul Jamil was asked, and said yes. I apologised to him and we did it again. As we were leaving we saw Abdul Fatah Younis in the lobby of the building. He had been a Major-General in Gaddafi's army and had been among the first of the military men to switch sides. I showed my accreditation to one of his aides, who nodded me through.

'Excuse me General Younis. We're from MBC TV. Would you give us a few words on the military aspects of the civil war?'

'How long do you want?'

'Fifteen minutes would be great.'

He sat down in the lobby and the camera was set up. 'You ready?' Mohamed nodded.

We worked fast, rushed back to the feed point and thank God, the two interviews were fine. MBC now had good footage of their own, from the ground.

Then we did a story on the pilot's family. Everyone in Benghazi knew who 'the pilot' was. Gaddafi, whose forces were fighting their way east with some success, had been threatening to demolish the city and show no mercy to its inhabitants. There were air strikes. But a couple of his own pilots took off in army planes from Benghazi and attacked his troops and tanks, inflicting heavy casualties. One of the planes was hit by anti-aircraft fire. The pilot could have ejected, leaving it to crash on the city, but he didn't. Instead he kept it in the air as long as he could so that it descended in the desert. He was killed, but he died a hero for he had paid with his life for the survival of many others.

A Dutch crew caught his plane coming out of the sky, and once the footage was broadcast they gave it to his family. We met his father and his son, and the story coincided with the International Day of Child Victims of Conflict. I made a report on the family with the old man, showed the Dutch clip, and then the boy appeared live, on the morning show, holding the picture of his father.

That went well, but we had finished in Benghazi and had to go further west to find the action. The front line, where rebels and Gaddifi's troops confronted each other, was at this time shifting back and forth through Brega, a 150 mile drive down the coast. The town was believed to be in rebel hands though that could change at any moment. We needed to be there.

It was a fast road, across desert, and a taxi took us. We had driven for less than half an hour when Mohamed Alsouhidi snapped his fingers. 'We left the mic behind.'

He was right. We'd left the mic, with MBC's logo on it, in the hotel after the live interview.

'We have to go back,' I said. This was one mission where everything seemed prone to misfortune. We returned, set off again, drove right across the desert, and through Adjabiya, and forty miles further, and stopped. We were outside Brega at a point where a crowd of TV and radio crews from all over the US and Europe had parked up and were pestering any any likely-looking ruffian with a weapon and a headband to let them get into town.

'What's going on?' I asked a French guy.

'CNN and Al Jazeera only. They're not letting the rest of us in.'

I called Dubai and explained. I said 'You'll get your report. I'll get something. Not sure what yet, but I'll let you know.' The hyped-up rebels, scruffy fellows with guns, were shouting around us. They started getting tough with us, trying to make us move back. A convoy of cars and vans was moving slowly through. Suddenly I spotted General Younis in one of the cars. I caught his eye and he lowered the window.

'You have a problem?'

'They're not allowing us through. Al Jazeera's OK, but not us.'

He stopped the car. He said to the rebels crowding round 'Why d'you let Al Jazeera go in and not these people? They're MBC, let them pass.' There was a muttered conference.

'OK, MBC can go.'

We drove on, and were in Brega. It isn't a proper town. It's a straggle of a place, more like a vast industrial site on an endless plain of sandy dirt. We could hear heavy shelling ahead and see smoke rising from the highway beyond, where the tarmac curved away towards the coast. Mohamed set up beside the road and we interviewed a couple of locals. I leaned down to our driver's window.

'Can we go on a bit further, so we get more shelling in the background?'

He shook his head. 'Too dangerous. I'm not going up there. Sorry mate - I've got a wife and kids.'

'We'll have to pack up,' I told Mohamed. 'This is as far as he'll take us.'

Because we'd been filming, we'd gathered a handful of people.

'I'll take you if you want,' a man said. He was a paunchy fellow who wore his blue shirt hanging over his trousers like a pyjama top.

'You've got a car?'

'Yeah, that one, up there.' He nodded twenty yards up the road at an old yellow Mercedes, parked, with a lot of stuff in the back. I looked at Mohamed and Majdi.

'What d'you think?'

'OK,' said Mohamed.

'All right,' I said. 'We'll do it quickly, just a piece to camera. You stay here,' I said to Majdi. 'We'll be back in half an hour.' I left him standing there with the tripod, ran back to the taxi to get my bag and ssqueezed into the front seat next to Mohamed. The guy drove us away, along the road.

There was one car ahead of us. We were soon in open desert, where there were no buildings at all. The driver picked up speed. Smoke rose into the sky and the gunfire was louder - but now it was to our right, and we seemed to be passing it. Our driver just stepped on the gas. The driver ahead waved him past.

We rounded the curve. Facing us, near a non-descript wayside settlement, stood a crescent of about thirty men, motionless, in army uniform, with a Libyan flag.

'Hell.' I murmured. Stopping crossed my mind but I knew it was too late. They'd open fire if we even hesitated now. And we didn't. We were approaching the soldiers. 'I can talk us through this,' I thought.

I looked at Mohamed. His face had turned grey. Our car was slowing down. The soldiers with guns were forty feet away, and walking towards us from both sides. Most of them looked like scared boys.

'Hacene,' said Mohamed 'I'm dead.'

Chapter 15

Solidarity

'Don't worry.' I wished I hadn't said that. I tried again, in an even lower voice. *'Don't panic.* I *know* these people. Have you got ID?'

He said nothing, but moved his head slightly to indicate No.

The car had stopped. The driver did not move. A tall, older soldier in immaculate uniform stepped forward and pulled a door open.

'Get out. All of you.' Mohamed and I got out. The driver didn't move.

'Hands above your head. Lie flat on the ground.'

We dropped to our knees and then onto stony ground.

'If they try anything shoot.'

We were side by side with our faces in the dust and I heard someone else getting down on my other side. It was Majdi, the bloody Egyptian.

'What the hell are you – ' I hissed.

He whispered 'I thought you'd need the tripod so I got in.'

He'd squashed next to the rubbish in the back seat. So now I was responsible for one Libyan, aged 26, and one Egyptian. If they found out Mohamed was a Libyan from rebel-held territory I didn't want to think what might happen.

We lay in silence. The ground was dry, chalky white pebbles. The Libyan Army had now got the Thoraya, our tapes, our personal cash, the MBC float which was supposed to provide our per diems and living expenses for the journey, my British press card, my bag, the camera. And the damn tripod. My passport, along with my credit cards, was in a safe at the hotel in Benghazi.

'You'll be OK,' I whispered to Mohamed.

'You picked me up in Alexandria, OK?' he whispered back.

'Yes.'

'I am based there.'

The soldiers were about twenty feet away, muttering to one another. I shifted my head to face Majdi.

'He is from Alexandria,' I whispered.

'OK'.

The soldiers were on the whole just hanging out. I couldn't see what they were doing here, unless they were a scouting party.

We must have lain there for about fifteen minutes. Finally the tall officer had us brought, one by one, to stand in front of him. I was last. The yellow Mercedes had gone, I noticed.

'Who are you?' the guy said.

'Hacene Zitouni from MBC.'

He took out a mobile phone. Looking at me as he spoke into it, he said 'Big fish for you here, guys. TV journalist, says he is British of Algerian origin. And two guys with him, one Egyptian, one Libyan, claims he lives in Alexandria. None of them's got a passport. All under arrest.'

A four-wheel drive came. Majdi was put in front passenger seat with a soldier and the driver, and Mohamed and I were in the back with the officer. The soldier took all our bags and equipment and put it in the back of the car.

They drove us to a military base full of middle-aged men, career soldiers in Gaddafi's army. We waited in a bare room for a a few minutes. My accreditation card, plainly issued by the rebels and not the army, was on a string round my neck. I slid it from its clip, folded it, popped it into my mouth, chewed and swallowed.

Our bags, the camera and tripod were offloaded into the building and piled on a bench outside the room. Through the door into the hallway, I could see an old soldier rifling through my bag, stuffing the pockets of his uniform with the $8,000 in cash.

'Hey,' I said. He looked up. 'That's mine,' I said. He looked up, stared at me and carried on foraging. Then he left; I never saw him again.

A soldier hurried in. 'Come on. You two, come with us.' He was waving a rifle at Mohamed and Majdi and pushing them out of the door.

Then another officer, not the tall one, came.

'Mr Zitouni.'

'Hallo.'

'Sit down, Mr Zitouni. You know Libya. You have been here before. What's an Algerian doing here?'

'Working for MBC with my team. Where've they been taken to?'

'You want to see them?'

'Yes.'

Mohamed and Majdi were brought back and told to sit down. A soldier appeared with bottles of Fanta, bananas, and dates on a tray. The officer said -

'You know that the officer who arrested you is a cousin of General Gaddafi?'

'I didn't know that.'

'He would like to talk to you again. He will be here in a minute.'

The tall one came back. 'You must leave your colleagues here, Mr Zitouni,' he said. 'You are coming with me.'

'But why can't we –'

'Never mind why.'

I didn't have much choice. I got into the back seat and they drove back to the point where we'd been arrested. The soldiers were still doing nothing in particular. He took me into a small dark concrete building.

'Sit down there.' There was an ammo box. I sat on it.

'I've had a phone call,' said the tall officer.

'But –'

'Nothing will happen to you or your colleagues. For the moment you are safe.'

I sat there for a while, staring through the entrance at the soldiers in sunshine outside.

'Just as a matter of interest,' I said 'why aren't you attacking the rebels?'

'No cover,' he said. He pointed at the sky. 'We're stuck here. If we had air cover we could move. But we don't, and if you move a body of men you get bombed by American planes. Or French or British - I don't know who, but they're all hostile. This is why I want to destroy those people,' he added, with a murderous look in the direction of Benghazi.

He went away. I sat staring into space, trying to make myself believe that Mohamed must by now have convinced his captors that he was based in Egypt and just doing a job.

The officer returned.

'You're coming with us now. We're taking all of you to Sirte.'

Sirte is closer to Tripoli. Everybody knew that Gaddafi had been born there and it was firmly in Government hands.

They drove me back to the military base and made me stay in the vehicle with two uniformed guards and a driver. Shortly afterwards Mohamed and Majdi were walked towards us at gunpoint with their hands on their heads. They were put in the back and I was moved to the front beside the driver. We set off.

'You don't remember me do you?' the driver said. He didn't look familiar. 'You came to the African Summit. You have been in Libya many times. Why did you come through Egypt?'

The tension lessened. I didn't risk turning to speak to the other two because they were silent and I thought there must be a reason. Only later did I find out that they travelled all the way with their hands on their heads while a guy had his gun trained on them. And sitting behind me the driver, another soldier had me in his line of fire.

We arrived at Sirte, where officers from military intelligence were stationed in a smart five-storey building. One of them was Colonel Abdul, a black guy I'd met a long time ago in Tripoli, when I'd visited with a Saudi delegation that came to discuss Lockerbie.

'Why did you put yourself in this position, Hacene? Why not come in through Sirte? You are always welcome here.'

'All journalists try to cover both sides. And your Government doesn't let us in through Tunisia. Anyway a lot of media people come here from Cairo. That's why.'

'It's the wrong way.'

'I'm only here to show what's going on, so I don't see that it matters which way I come in. I don't side with you or the rebels just because I came in one way or the other. I accept the sovereignty of your country, I don't need a visa, I'm Algerian.'

'You came in with your Algerian passport?'

'Yes,' I said.

'Where is it?'

I gave him the name and phone number of the hotel in Benghazi.

Mohamed got very different treatment. They said his clothes were Libyan and why should they believe his story about living in Egypt? At one point a soldier slapped him in front of me. They called him a traitor. I thought they were going to finish him that night.

They took us up a lot of stairs and put us together in a bare room with three bunks and a small shower and toilet enclosure, not particularly clean. They brought us our bags, and some food. All of us had had our money stolen. We spoke in near-whispers in case the room was bugged. Mohamed had given a street address for his non-existent family in Alexandria.

They took the trays away, and we slept. Next day nobody came. We had a window and a balcony. We were on the fifth floor, looking out onto pleasant gardens with palm trees and a big car park. There were other office buildings in the complex.

A young soldier unlocked the door at around ten in the morning.

'Have you had anything yet – fruit, coffee?'

'No. But that doesn't matter. When are you going to release us?' I took the role of spokesman. I was determined to be civil but as firm as I could without offending anyone.

'I don't know anything about release,' he said. 'I've only got to get your breakfast. Wait.'

He left. *'Wait?'* said Majdi. 'What else does he think we can do?'

He brought tea and biscuits for the three of us.

An hour later the same soldier came back.

'You're going to Tripoli today.'

We waited again. Then an officer came in. 'Come with me. Bring your things.'

'Where are we going?'

'First of all to Colonel Abdul's office. Hacene you're going to be on TV. Are you OK with that? We've got Hanan Halil to interview you, you know her?'

'No.'

'She is very well known on Libyan TV.'

'What's the interview about?'

'Nothing special, just how you came into the country.'

'OK.'

We all followed the officer, and an armed soldier brought up the rear. Lights and camera had been set up in Colonel Abdul's spacious office, and a sound man was standing by with a mic on a pole. Hanan Halil, when she turned up, was a forty-something with blonde streaks not quite concealed by her hijab, and a familiar face. I'd seen her on news reports bragging about Gaddafi's massive popular support.

We took our positions. Two secret service guys were sitting next to me but off camera, listening. She sat facing me and I could dimly see Majdi and Mohamed sitting with guards on a sofa, against a far wall behind the camera.

'How did you come into Libya, Mr Zitouni?'

'From Cairo.'

'And you came for MBC.'

'Of course.'

'How do you feel about media coverage of events in Libya?'

'I'm afraid it's been several days since I saw any coverage.'

'But you have seen reports from MBC and Al Arabiya before that...'

'Yes.'

'... so you'll have noticed the bias against our Government. What did they expect you to say about the situation here?'

'Expect me to say? I don't understand.'

'What did they tell you to say?'

'Madam,' I said. 'In twenty years I have never been told what to say. I have been to many conflict zones and nobody has ever said "go and blacken the name" of this side or the other.'

'And yet MBC persistently diminishes the success of Colonel Gaddafi who has led our country since 1969.'

'You must be thinking of other channels. MBC does not have an agenda.'

'So why do you report the disturbance here as if the Government is the aggressor?'

'I report aggression on both sides. I do not want to call attention to people killing each other but that is where we are.'

'But you came in from rebel-held territory, and naturally Government forces have detained you, and they have not treated you badly.'

'Not me, no.'

'If you thought Colonel Gaddafi was so determined to make trouble why did you risk falling into Government hands?'

'There's a conflict. It's my job to be here. I could just as easily have come in from Tunisia and then I might have been arrested crossing to the rebel side.'

The interview concluded with polite enquiries about Algeria and my family. And then they wrapped up.

'Now,' said the officer who brought us 'you are going to Tripoli.'

We were told to bring our bags and taken to a minibus. We three were told to sit in a row behind the driver, who sat smoking in the front seat. Behind us we were aware of other prisoners, two men, and a dishevelled woman with a black eye. The tall, broad-shouldered man, and the woman, started swearing in English at the guards who brought us. I thought they were Americans. The other man was silent.

The minibus did not move. The air conditioning was off and it was hot. The driver got out, locked us all in and had a word with the soldiers who'd brought us. They were watching us with a trigger-happy air and the driver went into the building, presumably for a toilet break.

I turned briefly and saw that the tall American had blood on his shirt and he and the woman had their hands tied behind them. The other man, I couldn't see, because he was immediately behind me.

'Hi,' I said to the American, turning away again to face forwards, so that it wasn't so obvious to people outside the car that we were talking.

'Hi.'

The woman said from behind me 'I'm Clare. That was James, and Manu's behind you. Who are you?'

'Hacene Zitouni. Can you hear me if I talk like this?'

'Yes.'

'You're all Americans?'

'Manu's Spanish,' James said. 'We're journalists. Are you press as well?'

'I report for MBC TV. I'm an Algerian from Britain and Majdi and Mohamed are from Egypt. Majdi's the producer and Mohamed's the cameraman. Have they taken your things?'

'Everything. Camera, laptop, money.'

'Same with us. A TV camera. Where were you arrested?'

'The front line outside Brega. They shot our friend.'

'A Libyan?'

'No. South African. They were firing at us. They didn't know we were press.'

'Where is he now?'

There was a pause. Clare said 'We don't know. They were firing and he fell.'

'Are you all from the same newspaper?'

'We're all freelance. Look they're coming.'

There was a move in our direction. Soldiers got in through the door at the back and an officer sat in the front next to the driver. We set off.

'Hey,' James shouted at the officer.'You gonna take these fuckin' cuffs off us or what?'

'Too fuckin' right,' said Clare.

There was no reply.

I turned round to him. I said - 'If you shout and swear - these people may speak English as well as you. You're not helping your case.'

'What the hell are we supposed to do then?'

'Nothing. Just keep quiet. These people have got orders. They are just doing their job. You don't need to antagonise them. Just shut up. They're not stupid. They may even sympathise but you're in their hands now.'

There was silence.

Clare said. 'I guess we've run out of other options.'

Tripoli is about four hundred kilometers from Sirte and the journey took a long time. James, who was in his thirties, was on an assignment commissioned by *The Atlantic*, the online version of *Atlantic Monthly*, which is one of the oldest and most respected periodicals in America. Clare was reporting for *The Atlantic* and *USA Today* and Manuel Brabo had been sending despatches to a Spanish newspaper.

The guards were fine with us. We stopped and had tea and almonds. (Libyan almonds are delicious.) They took the bindings off the others' hands and gave us all bottles of water. On the road, we three talked to the young officer and the even younger driver in front, about the war, and what was going on in Libya. I don't think we learned much. There was caution on both sides. But in our situation, I thought the best thing to do was keep tension low.

We got to Tripoli after dark, probably around 8.30pm. The city was lively; people were strolling along boulevards near the sea, the shops were open and brightly lit and it didn't seem that the shooting war was having any impact at all. There were military vehicles on all the busiest roads, and the people in front had to show documents more than once when we were stopped, but that was it.

They ferried us to a prison, but were told to move on to some other place. That wouldn't accept us either. They didn't seem to know what to do with us so they tried again, a place that looked like a big office complex in a garden. We got out and stretched our legs.

'What's this place?' I asked.

The officer said 'Nothing to worry about. We're taking you to secure accommodation but the jails are all too rough for journalists. And you've got the woman.'

We hung about for an hour while some invisible functionary made a decision. Then - and it must have been eleven at night by now – we were put back in the bus, and driven through big gates, where we again got out, close to a big old American van with windows, like a prison van. A different, and altogether more taciturn, set of soldiers blindfolded us, and shoved us into it at gunpoint. The walls inside were cold metal. I heard soldiers climbing in with us and slamming the door. One of them, who must have been an officer, banged on the side and shouted a sharp order to drive.

We set off. I could still hear soldiers shouting in the distance. The blindfold smelled bad and was painfully tight. I could feel the blood pounding in my temples and my eyes hurt with the pressure. I said in Arabic - 'This hurts my eyes. Could you loosen it please?'

'Who are you?' said a hostile voice.

'Hacene Zitouni from MBC TV.'

'*Tighten it,*' he told somebody beside me. It was agony. For the first time I lost confidence. Journalists disappeared. It happened all the time. *It could happen to me.* Charm and politeness did not always work. I tried not to think about Mohamed. I thought about Atlas. His birthday was two weeks away. I was taking him to see Real Madrid *vs* Barcelona. I'd promised him.

I tried to listen instead of thinking, and was sure, from the reverberation and the occasional military sounds, that we were driving around, not on a main road, but in a compound. When I understood that was an obvious and clumsy attempt to confuse us I regained confidence. These people were making it up as they went along. They were volatile. Being inoffensive was the only option.

The whole episode probably lasted no more than ten minutes, and when they stopped, took the blindfolds off and got out of the van, leaving us inside, I could see were in a barrack square lit by the dimmest of overhead floodlights, presumably so that it wouldn't be a target for bombers. Soldiers were talking outside. James started cursing.

'Keep quiet, I'm trying to listen.'

I heard

'Six? Journalists? Absolutely not. This is high-risk only. Politicos, not journos.'

'We've got to keep them somewhere. There's a woman with them.'

One of them looked up. He must have seen me duck down because they all moved away and in a minute they piled into the van again.

'Put their blindfolds on again,' the officer ordered.

'Where are we going?'

'Somewhere else.'

We got another ten-minute tour of the compound and out through the gates, and stopped. They pushed us down into the dark and hustled us at gunpoint over to the familiar people carrier, the one that had brought us from Sirte. They put us in that. The original officer and driver drove us away.

'Relax. We're taking you somewhere else because you're media. You can take those things off.'

We all took our blindfolds off and I kept mine. Funny how relieved we were to be in the people carrier; it felt almost safe, now. We drove in silence through the lively city again and were taken back to the office complex.

It wasn't an office complex, though. The corridors and rooms were bare concrete. The cell we were put into was windowless and dirty, with stained walls, three bunks and some bedding that demanded minute inspection before use. There was a modesty panel on the corridor wall and behind it, a squat toilet and a grubby, rusting shower; no soap or towels. The only natural light came from a plastic-covered skylight above the shower.

I was tired. All I wanted was sleep. As I dozed off I thought 'We're here for interrogation.' I only had one secret to keep, and I would.

Chapter 16

Mysterious workings

Early in the morning we heard low, regular thuds, like muffled knocking from one of the side walls. There was a rectangular plastic 3-pin power socket at waist height on every internal wall, and last night Mohamed had looked at them, frowned at me and said in a low voice

'D'you think they're bugs?'

I'd already rejected that thought. 'Doubt it. These people have got a war on. Nobody'd have time to listen.'

So Majdi knocked back and we all sat in silence. A voice said quietly

'Pull the socket away from the wall.'

With his fingernails, Majdi prised the socket fractionally clear of the plaster, tugged and the whole thing came away easily. It had been removed before. There was no wiring there at all; just a hole. He bent down and peered through.

'It's just dark,' he said, straightening up.

'Go back in the room,' whispered the voice. Majdi stood aside and I crouched a meter from the wall and peered through the hole. The man in the next room was doing the same, and I knew his face. I went closer to the wall and spoke in a whisper too.

'You're on TV,' I said.

'Yes, I work for Al Alam.'

Al Alam is an Iranian station and he was their correspondent in Canada.

'How long have you been here?'

'Twenty-two days.'

Our hearts sank.

This man - his first name was Iraj – had been arrested on the border with Tunisia, and had been filming without authorisation in cities as he came through. We spoke for only a short time before nervously replacing the socket.

And we waited. There were no books, and nobody felt much like talking. I didn't want to know Mohamed's true story and the implication of that was, I must not know anything about Majdi either. If I could go into detail about Majdi, then they'd think I could do the same about Mohamed.

All Majdi and I would know, if they asked, was that Mohamed came from Alexandria and he lived with his mother and his sister.

'Have they asked you for your address there?'

'No. I only know the main streets.'

Majdi said 'Say Building 4, Fish Market Street. I can tell you what it looks like round there because it's where my cousin lives.' Majdi described it.

They came and brought us something to eat at lunchtime. That afternoon, I was made to stand up and a blindfold was put around my eyes; a hand then grabbed my upper arm and I was taken away, into a lift going down, I don't know how many floors. Then along a concrete floor, turning right or left at command, until I heard a door shut behind me and I was pushed into a chair. The blindfold was taken off and I found myself in a plain room facing a man in a chair opposite. There was a single window high up behind his head.

'Why did you come here from Egypt?'

'Why did you not apply for permission to come to Tripoli?

'These men with you, who are they?

The same questions, over and over, for an hour, two hours, I didn't know. When I finally got back to our cell it was empty. Majdi and Mohamed came later. They too had been interrogated.

We thought James and Clare and the Spaniard were in another cell on this floor although we never saw each other. Sometimes I thought I heard American voices, one of them a woman's, but I was never sure.

On the second day, Iraj whispered through the hole

'All these sockets are to make you think they're listening, but I don't think they are. Could you knock on your other wall? I think there might be a team from Al Jazeera.'

We did what he'd done. We knocked, somebody knocked back, and we opened up. There was a Mauretanian cameraman, a Palestinian from Oslo, and an Egyptian producer.

A single guard patrolled every hour. We could hear him coming along the hall. He would stop and look in.

I began to worry that there was no sign of our release, and Iraj was now in his fourth week. My medication for diabetes and high cholesterol had been confiscated. I banged on the door and told the guard I needed it. He asked what for. He said he would ask somebody to find it for me.

Some days, the guards came at six in the morning for us and some days they didn't come at all, or they came for only one of us. Some days there were two intelligence officers to question me, and some days only one; different ones all the time. But every time, the same questions, over and over. The corridor was patrolled regularly, and the guard looked in, and we could hear him coming. But when, or if, we would be taken for interrogation we never had any idea.

The worst question for me and Majdi was always 'When did you meet the cameraman?'

I knew that they were looking for any excuse to kill him. I felt responsible for him because I had made the decision to go forward and I felt guilty. But we had to hold onto our story. He came as a freelance cameraman. We must keep repeating the address. None of us ever hesitated yet sometimes they took a long time with Mohamed, and he had bruises.

They gave us rice with sauce some days; the rest of the time, our diet was mostly bread. I kept asking for coffee and Majdi wanted cigarettes. They said 'Soon' but nothing ever happened so we started asking daily. After days of this, when nothing arrived, we banged on the door for attention. The guard's footsteps approached.

'If you keep banging on this door you'll get nothing at all.'

I said 'We're journalists. We've answered your questions honestly. You know we're not guilty of any crime. We need to be in a hotel.'

The footsteps receded. That day, the repeated questioning continued, with two interrogators in the room. The army had confiscated, besides my money, my mobile phone. On this were the names of certain opposition leaders with their numbers in London. I don't suppose any of these were news to Libyan intelligence, but they had a different angle anyway.

'How you get all these numbers?'

'I'm a journalist! We all have them. Some are Tunisian opposition, some are – there are all sorts of politicians, not just Libyans - there is no question of taking sides; it's my job to show every point of view. Your issue is your issue not mine. It's your country.'

'When these people are live on TV with you, do you pay them?'

'No. MBC pays a standard £70 appearance fee. They have to, it's something to do with British tax.'

'They are opposition!'

'So? That's got nothing to do with it. They have to be paid £70, that's the law in England.'

If you tell a refutable lie or behave weakly, they will take advantage of you because they are bullies. When they were ready to let me go I said

'I want you to do something, please.'

'To do what?'

'My colleagues and I are stuck here. We have nothing to tell you, we haven't done anything, so please let us go. Let us leave the country.'

'We can't do that. Anything else?'

'I want to call my family. I have my son in England, I want to call him, it's his birthday soon, he doesn't know where I am. And I want to call my mum in Algeria.'

'Is that the only request?'

'All right. It is the only request. Please, let me establish contact so that people know we are alive.'

A couple of days later they took me to the interrogation room and gave me a mobile phone. I called my mother, who was immensely relieved to hear my voice.

'MBC did a piece about you, they said you were missing. I am so glad you are safe. When will they let you go?'

'Not long now I hope. We are not charged with anything.'

I rang Tanya.

'Thank God you're OK. Somebody rang from the Foreign Office yesterday but I didn't say anything to Atlas.'

'What did they say?'

'Only that you'd been arrested but they didn't know what for. What are you supposed to have done?'

'Nothing. We haven't done anything except cross their border and we were waved through anyway. I'm sure they'll let us go soon.'

Some days after this I was as usual blindfolded and taken from the cell for questioning. It was about midday. In the interview room sat two men who had questioned me before. One of them, the younger one, spoke.

'You are well?'

This was a surprising start. 'I still don't have my medication.'

'It has been lost, Mr Zitouni. Many apologies for that. Otherwise you have been well treated? You have not been tortured?'

'No, I have not been tortured.'

'Would you like to leave?'

'Obviously. And I want the money that was stolen from me.'

'We know nothing about that except what you have told us. You are free to go. A car will collect you. Your things will be brought to you.'

I must not fall for this. 'And my friends?'

'In due course.'

'When? I won't leave without them.'

'I am afraid you must.' He nodded at the guard who had brought me.

'I'm not going,' I said.

I was escorted outside the room and made to sit on a bench. The guard stood next to me. The older interrogator emerged from the room.

'I'm not leaving without the others,' I said.

'Listen.' He sat beside me on the bench. 'You can do more good for your colleagues from outside this place. You can tell their families where they are and that they're OK. If we have to say that you've refused to leave, believe me, you will be stuck here for I don't know how long. And their families won't know anything.'

I said nothing. I could see the logic of what he said. The guard brought my bag and the medication. When he had gone the man said

'Agreed?'

I still said nothing because a battle was taking place in my mind.

'Good,' he said, getting up. 'This place is gone, it's over, so use your contacts.'

He left, and I sat hoping that he meant what I thought he did: that Gaddafi had effectively lost.

A car arrived, with two young men in cheap suits in the front seats.

'Lie down in the well of the car.' I did. The floor was dusty and smelled sour, but then so, most probably, did I; my clothes hadn't been washed for over a week, and I knew I stank of cigarettes. They drove and I lay in considerable discomfort on the floor, shielding my eyes from occasional flashes of penetrating sunlight. After a while the car slowed and the sides of trucks slid by, filling the car windows. Klaxons sounded more frequently. We were in the city.

'You can sit up now.'

I did. Never had a busy city looked quite so astonishingly lively; never had I felt, so poignantly, what imprisonment meant, and still meant to Majdi and Mohamed.

They drove, stopping and starting in traffic until we reached a souq. The driver turned around to face me.

'OK, we have our instructions - what you want to eat?'

'Nothing.'

'What do you want?'

'I want my colleagues to be brought out.'

'Can't help you there. Anything else?'

'I want you to take me to an hotel.'

'Hold on, we have our orders. First you go shopping. We will buy you clothes and shaving kit or whatever you need.'

'MBC does not allow us to accept gifts from anyone. I want my money. My money was stolen in front of my eyes. It was about $8,000 and if you give me that I can buy anything I want.'

'We can't give you that. We've got a packet of money to spend on you. Come with us, you can't wear the same shirt forever.' So both of them took me into the market, and I bought razors, after-shave, toothpaste, and shower gel. I had to get all my clothes laundered so I bought a pair of jeans. It was odd, having one's minder pay. I remember thinking that this was how a Sheikha must feel as she stalks around Harrods pointing at things, while a burly fellow with a bag of cash settles up as she leaves.

'You need more than just jeans. Come on, we've got a lot of money to spend on you.'

'How much?'

The guy showed me the packet of money he had. I decided that Gaddafi owed me for time, danger and distress, and bought a leather jacket and a suit. We put the bags in the car and they took me to the Corinthia Hotel. One of them collected a room key from the desk and gave it to me. They then left, telling me to wait, in the foyer, with my shopping bags because somebody was coming to talk to me. Sure enough, Moussa Ibrahim, Gaddafi's spokesman, turned up.

'We're terribly sorry about your arrest. Is there anything you need in the immediate term?'

'Double expresso, please.'

We had a coffee and I told him about Majdi and Mohamed and how important it was to get them out. He said he would try his utmost.

'The Egyptian is not the problem. It is the Libyan.'

'He lives in –'

'Whatever. Hacene there is an issue about which you're unaware. The driver of the car you were travelling in, at Brega, was arrested. That car was full of explosives. If someone had hit it, none of you would be alive.'

'Is that what they're telling you? Well I don't buy that. I don't think that driver was on the opposition side at all. I think he was sent by your lot to find a gullible journalist and bring him across the line as a warning. He found me. If I hadn't taken that lift from him Majdi and Mohamed wouldn't be in jail now. I'm responsible for them, you must see that. They're young guys. I hope you can do your best.'

I went to my room. The following day, some people from the Algerian Embassy visited me and I spoke to the Foreign Affairs spokesman on the phone from Algiers. 'Be careful,' he said. 'We've done all we can. We intervened to get you out.'

I thanked him and asked him if he could help get the crew released. He said 'Don't worry. You can talk to the Libyans about them yourself, now that you're out.'

There were, in fact, a lot of Libyan government people in the hotel. I recognised in particular their Ambassador to London, whom I knew. I approached him and explained. He already knew about Majdi and Mohamed. Like Moussa Ibrahim, he had heard about Mohamed and his claim to be based in Egypt. He made no promises. And then, somebody said 'Hacene! How are you?' and it turned out to be Khaled Kaim, Gaddafi's Deputy Foreign Minister, who had, in days gone by, been a friend of mine in London. I told him about Majdi and Mohamed as well.

'Their release is not in my hands Hacene. It's up to military intelligence services. It would be very difficult for me to intervene. I'll try but... At least you know they're not being badly treated.'

I knew no such thing, but I wasn't going to go round making accusations about beatings for fear of making matters worse.

A few days later, Khaled approached me again. 'I have good news for you. Majdi and Mohamed have been transferred to a hotel. Not this one, obviously, but - they're in a hotel.' I think he believed it.

Every day, developments, updates, gossip in the foyer - you were never quite sure of the truth of anything. I heard one night that Heads of State from sympathetic countries such as South Africa and Mauretania had arrived at the Corinthia intending to meet Gaddafi and encourage him to leave, under cover. If so, nothing came of it.

I hadn't talked to any Americans about Mohamed and Majdi; just about James Foley, Clare Gillis and Manuel Brabu. I was introduced to a woman journalist from *Atlantic* who was interested. 'We're getting so many different stories. Did you meet them?'

I told her I had, and she asked me to talk via Skype to people at the magazine in Washington. 'Don't worry,' she added ' –the Libyans won't mind.'

'I wouldn't be 100% sure of anything here. I'm very happy to help but I don't want to do it sneakily. Set it up and I'll do it openly so it's obvious we've got nothing to hide.'

So she brought her laptop into the restaurant when we were having lunch and afterwards, she carried it into the lobby next to the restaurant and got a connection. She then called me. I was still at the table, finishing my coffee.

'OK - I'm coming right now.'

In the lobby, I talked on Skype to somebody in America, at the channel James worked for.

'Their families are desperate for news,' I was told. 'Clare's mother's distraught. So anything you know is helpful.'

'Well, we were together for only the one day and I haven't seen them since we were all taken to the military intelligence place,' I explained. 'But it's not a dungeon. They'll be in a cell together. I know they were ill treated when they were first arrested. You know what soldiers are like, they think everybody's a spy. But James and Clare were being treated as media when I saw them. The Libyans were careful to take us to the military intelligence compound and not a jail. Media are recognised as non-combatants.'

'So you think they are alive.'

'Yes, of course.'

'Yours is the first confirmation we've had. Do you know anything about Anton Hammerl?'

'Who?'

'I take it you don't. He's a South African photographer from England. He's gone missing. He was probably with them in Brega.'

I thought quickly. I didn't want to take hope away, and I didn't really know the answer. 'James did say he'd been with a South African photographer but they lost sight of him when they were arrested.'

That was as far as I wanted to go.

I was badly affected by all this, although I didn't admit it even to myself at the time; after all, I'd got out faster than the others, my food and accommodation were being paid for, and I was in a position to exert whatever pressure I could (which wasn't much).

I complained to one of the Libyan officials about MBC's missing $8,000, and he got me a form to fill in, but that money was never seen again. I still had no passport and no credit cards. I was trying everything to get Majdi and Mohamed released. Every time I saw Ibrahim - every evening, because he had a suite at the Corinthia - I asked him what progress there had been. One night he said

'You know you say MBC is not biased.'

'Yes,' I said cautiously. I guessed what was coming.

'Well, we'd like you to do a few reports for them while you're here - d'you think they'd be interested?'

The upshot of this was that I ended up sending film of a pro-Gaddafi demonstration to Dubai. And one or two other reports that pleased the rubbish Libyan régime although I don't suppose for a nanosecond that I converted anybody to Gaddafi's cause. Also, because Ibrahim tended to hang watchfully about while I was working, I was able to doorstep him live in the hotel and get him to promise to try and have Majdi and Mohamed set free.

On Wednesday 13th April MBC rang. They'd now broadcast several subtly pro-Gaddafi reports from me, and it was time to go. I couldn't agree more. I was getting nervous; if this carried on, pressure from the régime could only increase, and I was already in danger of putting myself on a hit-list. Also, I had made a promise to Atlas. The match was on Saturday and the likelihood of our making it together to Barcelona was slender unless I got out.

'I'd go in a heartbeat, but I haven't got my passport or any money.'

'We'll organise something.'

I was walking alone that afternoon down a street not far from the Corinthia when a guy rolled along beside me in his blue BMW, and stopped ahead. As I passed, the driver's window slid down.

'Hacene? One minute.' He gave me his card. I knew the name; he was an anti-Gaddafi lawyer. 'Jump in the car. I want to have a word.'

I sat in the passenger seat. 'Look,' he said 'you should get out of Libya. I advise you, I tell you, things are getting dangerous. I know you have no money.' He handed me an envelope. 'There's 200 dinars in there. You may need it - but whatever you do, insist on leaving the country.'

'OK.'

When I came back to the hotel I'd made the decision. I now had about $500 and could leave, if I had paperwork – and I wouldn't have to let Atlas down. But somehow I had to persuade Moussa Ibrahim to put my name on the list of those who were allowed across the Tunisian border. I went to my room, packed and showered. In the early evening I knew he'd be in his suite. I called.

'Would you mind if I dropped by for a private word with you?'

'Not at all. Come up now - you're just the person I wanted to talk to.'

We were on quite chummy terms, and I knew he wasn't alone in the hotel. He shared the suite with his German wife Julia, whom he'd met when they were both studying at Exeter University, and their daughter.

He and I sat in his private study over tea. I said 'I have to go, Moussa. MBC are insisting that I find a way to leave, and there's a bus to the airport in the morning.'

'Oh no!' he said - 'We can't let you leave now, in the middle of the uprising. You are accommodated, aren't you? And you know we can provide a cameraman.'

'Listen,' I said 'I promised my son eight months ago that we'd go to watch the Madrid-Barcelona game and it's this Saturday. It's his birthday. I've got the tickets.'

'My god Hacene, the country's being destroyed and you want to take your son to a football match!'

'Yes. Yes, I do. I love him very much and Saturday's his sixteenth birthday.'

We sat in silence. He looked sad.

'Moussa,' I said. 'How did you get into all this?'

He sighed 'Same way a lot of us did. Saif Gaddafi.'

'He found you the job?'

'No, nothing like that. Saif Gaddafi is persuasive. He came to London and he was full of how Libya stood on the threshold of change and reform. He spoke to students. We were the most favoured sons and daughters of Libya, he said, young and educated in the west, like him. Obviously we couldn't expect old people to change Libya for the better. We'd be the ones who led the struggle, from within.'

'It sounds quite revolutionary.'

'It was... flattering. But he was in London when he said this, remember.'

'What went wrong?'

He didn't answer at first. Then 'I'm sure we're on the right path,' he said. I felt sorry for him.

'You're committed to it,' I said. 'I am not. I have to go.'

'Fine,' he said. 'You'll be on the list.'

I went back to my room, packed, showered and ordered an alarm call and coffee for 5.30am.

Chapter 17

Moving

On Thursday 14th April 2011, I was outside the front entrance to the hotel, in the crowd waiting for the airport bus, at six. My plan was to fly, tonight, from Tunis to Cairo, where the local MBC office had obtained my passport and credit cards from the hotel in Benghazi and would deliver them to the airport for collection - and from there onwards to arrive in London tomorrow and pick Atlas up. I felt 80% confident that I would get out without a problem. The rest was hope.

Two buses arrived and we drove in convoy, with security vehicles ahead and behind, to the western border. The officials accepted my exit permit. And on the Tunisian side, MBC had acted rapidly and efficiently. Documents were waiting for me so I could get into the country and fly out again.

A local correspondent and cameraman from MBC Tunis were waiting to interview me. I said that Majdi and Mohamed had still not been released so I would continue to demand their freedom I could through all available channels. Then I spoke to Al Alam, who interviewed me about my contact with their correspondent, who was still detained by the military intelligence.

The MBC crew gave me a lift back to Tunis, where we arrived in the mid-afternoon. At the airport I was told that the only Cairo flight with empty seats left at 4am. However there might be a cancellation at 6pm on Egypt Air... I waited in the airport on standby, but by five o'clock I knew the flight was full.

I was desperate to get away. I had been stuck in one place for too long and I had to keep moving. Travelling, having an airline take responsibility for my existence, would displace all the worries of the last horrible month. There was a flight at 8pm to Rome, and a connection from there to Cairo at 10pm. I booked myself onto the Rome flight, waited at Rome Airport, flew to Cairo and arrived there at 2am. It was now Friday. MBC had sent someone to meet me, and I picked up my passport and cards from him and booked myself into a Novotel near the airport for 3 hours' sleep (a false hope; sleep failed to come). I was on the 8am BA flight from Cairo to London. I arrived at Heathrow late that morning feeling elated; finally, I knew I was away from that prison.

I put my things in my flat, and caught a train to Norfolk. I collected Atlas, brought him back on the train to London, went with him to Piccadilly to collect some funds that MBC had transferred to me via Western Union, returned to the office, got on the internet and booked an early morning flight to Madrid. We took rooms at a hotel near the airport, and before we set off for the game, I booked us onto a flight the following day - to Algiers, to see my family.

I had realised Atlas's dream. I hadn't let him down.

What did I learn from all this? Never to lose hope.

Also, always trust your instincts. If I'd trusted mine, I wouldn't have set foot in Libya in the first place.

And - not a new perception, but the reinforcement of something I already knew - media people may snipe and complain, but they stand solidly together in a crisis. After the holiday with Atlas, I returned to the normal daily round and was able to catch up with the huge network of news exchange and messages of hope that had been zipping across the world between press and broadcasting corporations and agencies, and the families of those detained. James, Clare, Manu and their missing colleague Anton were the focus of anxiety on three continents. David Bradley, owner of the Atlantic Monthly group of newspapers and online news magazines, was deeply concerned. People from Fox News were talking to people from the *Guardian*, the *Wall Street Journal* was in touch with Al Jazeera, and about thirty journalists representing every medium and political persuasion were emailing and copying-in between Europe, North Africa and the USA.

I found out almost immediately, from these emails, that Moussa Ibrahim had been telling the world that Anton Hammerl 'would be released.' I had not specifically discussed the South African photographer with him, but I definitely had the impression from what James and Clare said that he had probably died, or at any rate, been seriously injured, outside Brega.

However I was not certain of that outcome. So although the emails told me that his wife and young family were desperate for news, I told his wife the truth: that I didn't know. I gave her the phone number of a Libyan lawyer in London well connected to Qataris and Libyans. I spoke also to the Libyan Ambassador, although nothing came of it. It was possible that Moussa Ibrahim told the truth. Maybe Anton had recovered in a hospital somewhere and would soon be sent home. But common sense told me Ibrahim's source of news was military intelligence, who would think nothing of lying to him.

If I had felt uneasy in my captivity, I could not begin to imagine how Hammerl's partner must be feeling when she had heard contradictory information so many times in six weeks - and nothing at all that could be relied on. They had three young children.

At the beginning of May, a UN delegation visited foreign prisoners in Libyan jails and hospitals and the Hungarian Ambassador was allowed to visit Clare and James, who were sharing a cell. The authorities told him they'd be released 'within a week' and that Anton Hammerl was not in custody.

Clare Gillis was removed from the detention centre and sent to a women's prison. On 17th May, Ibrahim announced to AP that four foreign journalists, namely James, Clare, Manu and 'one other' had been before a judge in a courtroom and would be released 'soon'. The other, was the implicit hope, would be Anton Hammerl.

The Libyans were still allowing a trickle of ex-detainees to leave, although they had shifted their de-briefing of them, and hosting of media generally, from the Corinthia to the Rixos Hotel since I left. On 18th May the two Americans and the Spaniard were taken to the Rixos, free at last, along with a British journalist who was released by accident because of an administrative error. The South African Ambassador had turned up at the Rixos for the press conference. If he had gone with real hope of greeting Hammerl he was disappointed. He told journalists he didn't have any knowledge of the photographer's whereabouts. In the next few days, James would have the ghastly task of explaining Anton's fate to his widow. I did not envy him.

Many others remained in custody, including Majdi and Mohamed. Majdi was released in June, but Mohamed remained. I got in touch with the Red Cross, and I asked David Bradley for help. He said he had one idea which he would pursue for Mohamed.

Mohamed was finally released with the fall of Tripoli in August. I don't doubt that he had been ill treated. The Libyans had always discounted the story about Alexandria and treated him as a traitor.

After Libya I was left feeling nervous about going into conflict zones. Objectively, a few weeks in detention are insignificant. Subjectively, I was badly affected by the experience. It's about control; we all expect to be able to look ahead, and in that situation - the one in which Majdi and Mohamed still found themselves - you can't plan three minutes ahead. Your life is in somebody else's hands. And many journalists I have known have been killed.

So reporting from conflict-torn Syria with Islamic Relief was a test for me. The people in Dubai were surprised when I put my name down for the assignment but I was glad I went. I got my nerve back. For me, that's the fourth lesson: confront your fears. I would have been less sanguine, of course, had I known that just five months before my own visit to Idleb, James Foley had disappeared outside the town, believed kidnapped. That was in November, 2012, and as I write, in April 2014, his whereabouts are still unknown. In Libya, his nationality meant he was viewed as a spy. I don't doubt that the same applies in Syria.

Syria was my swansong as a foreign correspondent for MBC. Sheikh Walid Ibrahim, the owner, has decided to move its base of operations from Media City, Dubai to Media City, Jeddah. Frankly, if I had my doubts about working in Dubai, I sure as hell don't want to live in Jeddah, so that's the end of it for me. It marks a shift in Arab media as a whole: a closing down. Al Jazeera has had a bias towards the rebel side since the Arab Spring began; MBC Group was much the same. It has slowly, perceptibly withdrawn from the contest for news coverage and from now on, neither MBC nor Al Arabiya will even have their own foreign correspondents. MBC will be focussed on Saudi Arabia only. International news will be beamed from agencies abroad to Al Arabiya in Dubai, there to be commented on by journalists in the studios.

Cheap? Yes. (And cheaper still, the haggling over my final redundancy package.) But I feel jubilant: oddly liberated. I have taken an exam to enter a new and exciting profession. I am standing for public office. I am exploring an interesting option in television. From now on I can do whatever I like, without any concern for office politics or bullying employers.

You might think that as a TV reporter who felt his work mattered, I would carry on doing pieces to camera until I was as old as Walter Cronkite, who addressed a delighted American public for more than sixty years. Well, no. I have learned a lot about dealing with people, and I've told the truth. That's enough for me.

interviewing Ali Abdullah Salah Yemeni President in Sanaa 1995

With Soundman Abed in Cairo before going to Yemen

Eating 'Kat' in Yemen while covering the war

With British Prime Minister John Major at MBC New Headquarters in Battersea

Trying a camel Ride in Damazine- Sudan

With Former Sudan Prime Minster Mubarak Al Mahdi

In Al Ayoun covering the Western Sahara conflict with Morocco 2006

In Baghdad waiting for UN Press conference

In Dili - First Arab reporter to cover East Timor Conflict

Greeting Sulatan of Brunei Hassan Balkia

Interviewing Prince Salman during an official visit to Australia

at the famous Tiananmen Square Beijing, China

At the Great China Wall

With Hassan Al Turabbi - A controversial Sudanese
opposition leader at his office in Khartoum 1996

with Prince Sulatan Bin Salman and Ali Al Hedeithy
MBC C.E.O at the Great China Wall